Newtyle

A

Planned

Manufacturing

Village

by WILLIAM MURDOCH DUNCAN, B.Sc., A.L.A.

Published in 1979 by Forfar Historical Society

Printed in Scotland by
Wm. Culross & Son Ltd., Coupar Angus, Perthshire

DEDICATION

To ROSE ELIZA JEFFERY, who retired as postmistress
of Newtyle on 10 May 1961, and died on 8 October
1974 at the age of 73.

She was a magpie who collected literally everything
of a local nature, but especially photographs and
horse brasses. She gave her photographs to the village, and thus is responsible for starting this history.

CONTENTS

		page
Chapter 1.	Geography and History	1
2.	The Churches	23
3.	Social Life	29
4.	Education	38
5.	Work	53
6.	Transport	72
7.	Leisure	82
8.	The Games They Played	89
9.	Shops and Jobs	98
10.	Some Brief Biographies	103
Bibliography		107
Index		111

ILLUSTRATIONS

Front cover	Kinpurnie Tower: from the Newtyle Local History Collection
Frontispiece	Map of Newtyle Village, 1872
page 2	Map of Newtyle area, by Frank S. Benzies
,, 16	Hatton Castle
,, 24	The Parish Church 1767 and 1872: Drawings by the author
,, 66	32-Loom Factory: Weavers' Houses in Belmont Street: Drawings by the author
,, 68	Loomshops in North Street: Drawings by the author
Facing p. 72	First Railway Engine in Scotland
,, p. 73	Railway Station at Newtyle
,, p. 88	Chemical Works
,, p. 89	The Smiddy
page 100	John Jack's Workshop and Houses Rabbie Gray's Inn and the Poor-house: Drawings by the author
Inside Back cover	James Mackenzie's triangulation of Belmont Privy's Prap: Kinpurney Tower
Back cover	Privy's Prap on Keillor Hill: From the Newtyle Local History Collection

NOTE—The numbers in brackets throughout the text refer to the bibliography

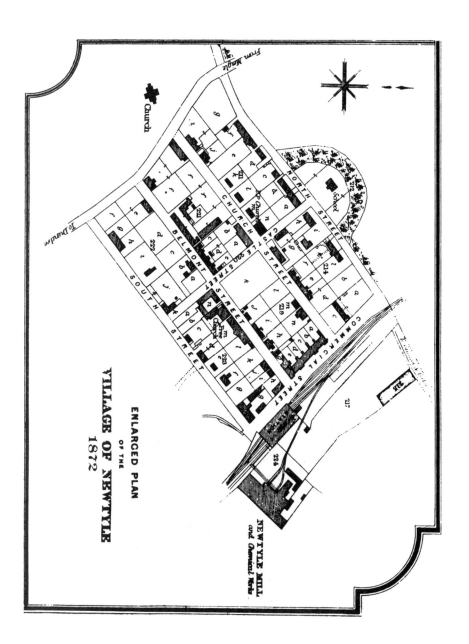

ENLARGED PLAN
OF THE
VILLAGE OF NEWTYLE
1872

PREFACE

As this historical account shows, Newtyle has been singularly fortunate in that it has always been able to breed and to attract people of outstanding ability. The account is full of such characters. William Duncan, its scholarly author (who also drew some of the illustrations), is one of that notable company.

In 1950 fate brought the author to Newtyle. Nearly 20 years later, after a successful academic career, he accepted an invitation from the Village Committee to make a collection of material relating to the railway, which from its opening in 1831 to its closure in 1964, had influenced Newtyle's development, particularly by linking the village to the industrial city and port of Dundee. That task led him to wider studies which culminated in this deeply researched story of a 'Planned Manufacturing Village.'

A community which forgets its history may be compared to a man who has lost his memory. As a result of William Duncan's labours the people of Newtyle and of its surrounding countryside need never suffer such deprivation.

The author deserves the most warm congratulations on the successful delivery, after 10 arduous years of gestation, of this remarkably worthwhile book.

JAMES BANNATYNE,
Bannatyne, Newtyle, Angus.

INTRODUCTION

This is the story of a small area, the old parish of Newtyle, eleven miles north-west of Dundee. It is told in depth. It is the story of people—of grannies and grandads—not of kings and queens (their story is well documented). In other words a social not a political history.

The story can never be fully told. Somewhere there is more information which may change ideas—the difficulty is to find it. There are some hearsay tales which are not easy to prove or disprove. Where they are given in the text they are stated as hearsay evidence. They are not ignored.

One legend of Newtyle is of the cannibal of Auchtertyre who was chased over the Sidlaws by a thousand men, captured and taken to be tried in Dundee. This legend is the figment of the imagination of James Grant in his novel *The Yellow Frigate*.

I have made few comments or deductions from the information found, mainly because the area is small and local. Comparison and correlation would have to be done with other areas, to make comment worth while.

My grateful thanks to individuals and libraries who have helped with information, printed and oral.

W.M.D.

USEFUL INFORMATION

Dates	Candlemas—2 February	Whitsunday—15 May
	Martinmas—11 November	Zuill (Yule)—25 December

Money	£1 Scots	=1s 8d English (at the Union) (now 8½p)

Measures	1 boll	=6 imperial bushels, or 140 lbs.
	1 imp. bush.	=2219·36 cubic inches or 1·28 cubic feet
	1 firlot	=¼ boll
	1 peck	=2 gallons or ¼ bushel
	1 firkin	=56 lbs or 9 gallons (brewing)
	1 lippie	=7 lbs.
	1 mutchkin	=¾ imperial pint or ¼ Scottish pint

Chapter 1

GEOGRAPHY AND HISTORY

Geology

Newtyle lies on the northern slope of the Sidlaws and looks northwards over the valley called Strathmore.

The Sidlaws themselves are igneous rocks—once molten and then solidified some 400 million years ago. The strath or valley of Strathmore is sedimentary and mostly Lower Red Sandstone. There is some evidence of an inland sea dating back to Devonian times (400m years ago) in the fossils found in and near Strathmore. One especially is the fossil fish *pterapsis mitchelii* found at Auchtertyre farm about 1880 [9]. Previously the only other example in Scotland was found at Bridge of Allan.

In addition there is a lot of river-borne sand in Strathmore. A dry windy day at Kirkinch can raise quite a sandstorm. The word 'Inch' (common enough in Scotland) means 'island' – another clue to the wet nature of the valley there. The Devonian sea had gone, leaving wet boggy ground to be drained.

The Glack or Pass of Newtyle is that part of the road between Dundee and Newtyle, just south of Newtyle where it crosses the Sidlaws. This was also very boggy, and on the west of the road there is evidence of the Ice Age left by the grinding of the ice as it moved. There is a similar feature at Tullybaccart on the Dundee to Coupar Angus road just south of Pitcur.

North of Millhole farm, off the Dundee to Newtyle road, there are two outcrops of rock known locally as the 'spec knowes' (spectacle mounds).

We find along the lower slopes of the Sidlaws a considerable number of quarries—some small enough to supply stone to build one single house or farm, and others larger. Burnside quarry was found to be extensive enough for large quantities of road metalling. Some of the quarries lower down were used to make stone tiles or tylds. These were used for roofing, and were mostly sedimentary or metamorphic rocks, e.g. sandstone or whinstone.

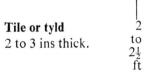

Tile or tyld
2 to 3 ins thick.

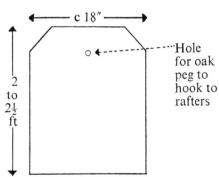

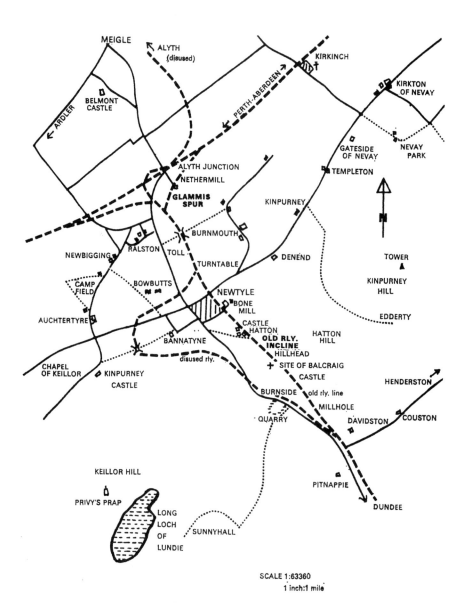

MEIGLE

ALYTH
(disused)

KIRKINCH

KIRKTON
OF NEVAY

PERTH-ABERDEEN

BELMONT
CASTLE

ARDLER

GATESIDE
OF NEVAY

NEVAY
PARK

ALYTH JUNCTION

NETHERMILL

TEMPLETON

**GLAMMIS
SPUR**

KINPURNEY

N

BURNMOUTH

NEWBIGGING

RALSTON
TOLL

DENEND

TOWER

TURNTABLE

KINPURNEY
HILL

CAMP
FIELD

BOWBUTTS

NEWTYLE

EDDERTY

AUCHTERTYRE

BONE
MILL

CASTLE
HATTON

**OLD RLY.
INCLINE**

HATTON
HILL

BANNATYNE

HILLHEAD

CHAPEL
OF KEILLOR

KINPURNEY
CASTLE

disused rly.

+ SITE OF BALCRAIG
CASTLE

HENDERSTON

BURNSIDE

old rly. line

MILLHOLE

QUARRY

DAVIDSTON

COUSTON

KEILLOR HILL

PRIVY'S PRAP

LONG
LOCH
OF
LUNDIE

SUNNYHALL

PITNAPPIE

DUNDEE

SCALE 1:63360
1 inch:1 mile

2

Early History

The *New Statistical Account* of 1842 mentions a souterrain at Auchtertyre being found within the 'last 40 years.' Guthrie [40] in 1875 states that 'some of those curious subterranean dwellings called weems or peghts' houses having been discovered about 60 years ago on the lands of Auchtertyre.' The Original Name Books of the Ordnance Survey [86] give it as 'about 7 chains S of Auchtertyre . . . under or near the statute labour road to Kettins . . . it was dug into some years ago and ashes were found . . .' About 1960 there was some memory of the souterrain having been seen about 1906 when Kinpurney Castle was being built and the road up to it widened. 'It seems to have extended under both Newtyle/Kettins road and the road to Kinpurney Castle and Pitcur, which suggests that its length was not less than that of a normal souterrain. Some part of it undisturbed by two road-making operations may possibly remain in the corner of the field.' [111].

When this area was being examined by Dr Wainwright in 1951 the plough was digging up large flat stones in the field at the north-west corner of the Auchtertyre/Pitcur and Newtyle/Kettins crossroads. No extensive digging has taken place.

Auchtertyre seems to have a lot of pre-history in it. There are signs of an earthwork in one of its fields. In 1928 Crawford [25] of the Ordnance Survey found part of a Stone-Age glass ball measuring about $\frac{3}{4}$ inch in that same field [6]. The ball was blue with yellow inlay. A bronze socketed axe also was found at Hatton farm about 1910 [7].

About 1949 two mounds were uncovered by deep ploughing in a field on the west side of the Newtyle/Meigle road, just north of the railway embankment. There is no doubt that these were graves, some 3 to 4,000 years old; but very little investigation was carried out. The mounds were known locally as the 'bow butts' probably because of their use in mediaeval times for archery practice. Hearsay has it that the bowmen attended the church leaving their bows and quivers at the door, then after the service practicing at the bow butts.

The Romans

The first *Statistical Account* of 1792 states that 'some traces of a camp' are visible in what is now a field, at Auchtertyre (mentioned above). The *New Account* of 1842 [101] speaks of 'evident remains of a camp of square form, and of no great dimensions,' adjoining Crewe Well in 'Camp Field.' The O.S. map of 1865 marks three of the four sides. Crawford [25] found slight traces suggesting a double ditch, each side measuring 350 feet. (So much for the 'no great dimensions' of the N.S.A.). According to Crawford 'inside the area enclosed is a mound on which aspen trees grow. The earthenwork is most unlikely to be Roman.' Tradition has it that the Marquis of Montrose and his army camped here during the civil wars. The Earl of Crawford from Fife is also supposed to have camped here. The nearest the Romans seem to have been is Cardean. A Roman coin was found at Pitcur in 1900—but it could have reached there in umpteen different ways.

Denoon—hill or castle of birds.

Another early site is known as Denoon Castle, but it is a hill fort. It is sited on Denoon Law about two miles west of Glamis. There is a good description with drawings and measurements by Christison in the *Proceedings of the Society of Antiquaries* of 11 December 1899 [6]. Little information has been noted since then, so the reader is referred to a good library for more detailed information.

The Keillor Stone

This is sited on the high road from Newtyle to Pitcur about a mile past the gates of Kinpurney Castle.

It is described as a Class 1 stone with wolf (sometimes called a bear), a double disc and Z-rod, with mirror. Its date is put at early Christian—7th or 8th century—but it could be earlier. It stands about seven feet high. After being broken just about ground level it was repaired about 1880. A drawing of this stone in John Stuart's book of 1856 [104] shows the carvings very clearly. That in the Bannatyne book of 1848 [10] is not so clear and not in the correct proportions. There is another drawing in Allen and Anderson's book of 1903 [1] with better proportions but less detail.

Warden [113] in 1880 just mentions 'the figure of an animal, below which are the spectacles and other symbols . . .' Other writers' comments shows the gradual wearing away of the gneiss stone until by the 1950s Taylor [105] simply says 'defaced' and leaves it at that.

It was not until 1974 when it was photographed by Dr Sandison at the right time and the right angle of the sun that the carvings show up as still being there.

There have been many discussions on the purpose of these standing stones. One suggestion is that they mark royal burial sites—certainly according to Warden [113] several cists containing bones have been found in the tumulus on which the stone stands, and 'ancient sepulchar remains have been found in the adjoining field.' Chalmers puts forward the view that this stone may indicate 'the ancient march of the great Earldoms of Strathearn and Angus.' It is certainly not far from the boundary line of Perthshire and Angus.

The word 'Keil' or 'Kill-aird' means a church or burial-place situated on an eminence. So the Chapel of Keillor may have been the site of some early place of worship and/or burial.

There is a stone in Meigle Museum, which is reputed by Patrick Chalmers to be noted in the *Extracta e Cronicis Scotiae** in 1569—

'At Newtylde thair is ane stane callit be sum the Thane Stane, iii eln of hecht, v quarteris braid, ane quarter thik and mair, with ane cors at the heid of it, and ane goddes next that in ane cairt, and twa hors drawand hir, and horsemen under that, and fuitmen and dogges, halkis and serpentis: on the west side of it, ane cors curiously grauit; bot all is maid of ane auld fassane of schap. It is allegit that the

*Translated, at the King's behest, from Latin to Scots by John Bannatyne (or Bellinden).

Thane of Glammis set thir tua stanis quhen that cuntrey was all greit forrest.'

(Daniel Wilson. *Prehistoric annals of Scotland,* 1863, p.233).

(Eln or ell=c 1¼ yards—it varies).

History up to the 18th century [113]

Sir William Olifaunt or Oliphant of Aberdalgie was a faithful adherent of King Robert the Bruce, and was one of the barons who signed the letter to the Pope. For this reason Bruce granted to Sir William a charter of the lands of Newtyle and Kylprony or Kinpurnie with 'all the liege and native men of these lands, performing the fourth part of a knight's service in the King's army.' It is dated at Newbotyll, 26th December, in the twelfth year of his reign (1317). (Historical Manuscripts Commission. 5th Report). When Neil of Carrick resigned into the King's hands the lands of Ochtertyre (which had belonged to John Comyn) Bruce gave these to Sir William in return for the service of three archers in the King's army—dated at Scone 20th March, 1326.

In 1364 Walter Oliphant (son of Sir William) resigned the lands of Newtyle and Kynprony to King David II, who confirmed them to the said Walter and his wife, Elizabeth (the king's sister) in return for a pair of silver spurs at the feast of All Saints at Haltoun of Newtyle yearly, 'in the name of blench farm with three suits at the king's court.' A similar charter of the same date, gave the lands of Ochtertyre and Balcraig, in return for three broad arrows on the feast of St Martin (Martinmas) at Ochtertyre in 'the name of blench farm with three suits at the king's court at Forfar.'

The blench feu duties were a curious form of land tax. The words 'all the liege and native men' show that the serfs were at that time slaves, passing from owner to owner when the lands were transferred.

In 1457, for some reason, and on instructions from the king, David Guthrie of Kingaldrum, Sheriff-Depute of Forfar, signed and sealed over, one-third part of the lands of Ochtertyre and Balcraig, and the mill, to William Hakate. Later in 1524 we find Elizabeth Aytoun, spouse of John Halket of Pitfirren, resigned her third part of Ochtertyre and Balcraig, in favour of Robert Marser of Mikillour. On 24th September 1508 before Andrew, Lord Gray, Sheriff of Forfar, a decision was made that the myre of Newtyle, between Newtyle and Auchtertyre, belonged to John, Lord Oliphant, and that the lands of Migill (Meigle) belongs to John, Earl of Crawford.

The family of Bannatyne (also recorded as Bellenden, Billenden and Ballantyne) must have acquired land in the 16th century, as we find that Thomas Billenden of Newtyle was appointed a Lord of Session in 1557 [131].

Balcraig is marked on the O.S. maps, as in one of the fields on Hatton farm, but other than this and mention in the Historical Commission's documents, there is no indication of such a castle.

The lands held by the Oliphants were:

In 1605 John, Lord Oliphant, grandson of Lawrence who built Hatton castle, held the barony of Newtyle and Kinpurney with the Mill of Newtyle; the barony of Auchtertyre and Balcraig.

In 1643 Patrick, Lord Oliphant (John's heir) was given the toun and lands of Pitnepie in the barony of Newtibber.

(The Oliphants were also proprietors of Turin, Drimmie and Gallery.)

The Oliphants kept possession of most of these lands until early 17th century, when they were acquired by the Hallyburtons of Pitcur, the first of them being Sir James Hallyburton. His son, William, owned the lands and barony of Newtyle, Kinpurney, Auchtertyre and Balcraig; the toun and lands of the Kirkton of Newtyle, and the toun and lands of Balmaw. They stayed in the possession of the Hallyburtons till shortly after 1681.

The croft or land of the vicar, or church lands of Newtyle, belonged to the Lindsays (Earls of Crawford) in the 16th century, and by 1596 we find them in the hands of Patrick Lindsay of Barnyards, at a feu of £11 (Scots).

The lands and barony of Newtyle, etc., were acquired by Sir George Mackenzie of Rosehaugh, and by 1691 George Mackenzie, son of Sir George, was in possession of:

the lands and barony of Newtyld and Kilpurnie, with mansion there of Newtyld (Bannatyne) and mill;

advocation of the church of Newtyld;

the lands and barony of Auchtertyre and Balcraig, with pendicles of same called Denend, Reidford, Newbigging, and Boghead;

the land of Bournemouth;

the lands of Clinsh in the barony of Auchtertyre and Newtyld;

the lands of Hillend or Templebank;

the lands of Hatton of Newtyld;

croft of land in the village of Hatton of Newtyld;

the toun and lands of Kirkton of Newtyld, and Brewlands;

the church lands of Newtyld with tiends;

some of the land of Balmaw;

the lands of Henderstoune, Sillieseat, Edderty, Newtibber, Pitnappie, Coustonne, Davidstoune, the Mill of Milnhole, and pendicle of Burnside;

the dominical lands and mansion of Wester Keillour; also Easter Keillor, in the barony of Lintrathen, Pitcur, Gask, Balgove, Balluny, Newton of Balluny, Balgillo, Eastounend of Keattins, Pitdounie, etc.

Up to about 1750 the owners of baronies in Scotland had the power to hold courts, which were overseen by an official known as the 'Baron-Bailie.' These powers could be considerable, even the right to inflict capital punishment. Appeals to higher courts were allowed, but seldom used. These Baron's courts were intended to enforce the conditions of a tenant's lease; to punish those who broke estate regulations; and to settle questions between tenants.

Sir George Mackenzie kept a 'Court Book of the Barroneys of Newtyld, Keillors, Couty and Bendochie begun in Anno 1725.' The first court was held 'at ye Milne of Newtyld 15th day of September 1725, by Patrick Grant of Bonhard, bailly yrto.' [12].

6

A court held at Haltown of Newtyld on the 8th November 1725 by Mr James Howry at Pitcur, who had become bailly, made the following appointments: Patrick Coupar, writer at Newtyld, Clerk to the Court; Thomas Murray in Kirktown, Procurator Fiscal; and Andrew M'Kewan in Kirktown, Ground Officer.

A number of Acts were promulgated that day 'for the good and advantage of the said Barrony.' They were ordered to be 'read publicly once or twice a year at the most frequent meetings of the tenants.' Some examples of these Acts are:

Tenants were forbidden to take possession of 'commontys' or common lands. Penalty £10 Scots.

Tenants were forbidden to cut trees or branches or to use any trees given to them 'but to the use of their bigings' (buildings). Penalty £10 Scots.

Tenants had to take their corn to the mills to which they were astricted. They must not take home farm meal until it went to the girnall (granary).

Tenants were not allowed to sell peats or to take a too great use of the moss.

Tenants were not allowed to 'resett or entertain' vagrants or allow them to reside in their 'grass-houses.'

Tenants were not allowed to break up sward ground (old grass).

Tenants must frequent the smiddy at Newtyle, and the blacksmith must give due attendance to them.

Tenants must not sow pease after oats.

Tenants must not frequent public houses and offices not authorised.

No one was allowed to set up an alehouse, a smithy or a maltbarn unless permitted by the master, but when permitted, tenants must frequent them.

Tenants had to deliver a certain amount of yarn between Zuill (Yule) and Candlemas. The best yarn was to receive a quantity of lint as a reward. The worst spinner to deliver double the usual quantity next year.

A court was held at Keillor on 31st May 1726 where a number of residents were sworn in as 'birleymen' (byrelawmen = ombudsmen) and a moss-grieve was appointed.

At the Court at Couty and Newtyle on 12th June 1733 James Allison was appointed factor by the Countess of Bute and her second husband, Lord Strichen.

At a Court held at the Milltown of Newtyle in 1736 certain tenants in Ochtertyre were forbidden to till the 'march balks betwixt their respective falls of ground' (the strips of grass ground separating one holding from another).

Sir James Kinloch of Kinloch at the Court at the Miln of Newtyle on 30th January 1740 complained about a number of persons taking peats from the Moss of Nevay. Twenty-three 'cartfulls' of peat valued at 9s Scots per cartful had been removed. Four honest men (they had owned up) had to pay Sir James 9s Scots per cartful plus £20 Scots damages between them.

At a Court held at the Miln of Newtyle in December 1756 the tenants were accused of not furnishing their several proportions of thatch for the schoolhouse.

(The Mill of Newtyle was sited where Milton house in South Street now stands).

Regulations were made at a Court at Newtyle in December 1770 regarding the use of marle; sowing of pease and grass; and making head-ridges adjoining roads (the practice had been to plough right up to the edge of the road, so damaging it).

In October 1770 George Watson (father of the famous Hugh) was appointed superintendent of the estates.

On 2nd January 1771, at Newtyle, two men were fined 5s and one fined 2s 6d for removing turf.

One interesting case came up at the Court of Kirkinch in September 1775, when several little children had set fire to the Moss of Nevay, adjoining the Moss of Drumkilbo. The children explained that they did this for their own diversion, and because other children had done the same on Drumkilbo. The parents were fined only 2s 6d each because of their poverty.

We find from the muster roll of the Forfarshire, or Lord Ogilvy's Regiment, raised on behalf of the Stuarts in 1745-6, that five men came from the Newtyle district [59]:

Joseph Ferguson, weaver, Chapel of Keillor.

David Mill, weaver, Newbigging of Newtyle.

Robert Ramsay, weaver, Balmaw, Newtyle.

David Yoully, weaver, Newbigging.

David Young, weaver, Newbigging.

All of them submitted after Culloden, and were sent home.

The new village

Before 1832 Newtyle was only a small hamlet or kirk toun, with Kirkton farm and cottages, and the smiddy and church, on the west side of the main road. Bannatyne house was a bit west of this, along with the mill and Bannatyne Home farm. The Mill of Newtyle was east of the main road, and gave its name to Milton house in South Street. There were at least two houses which stood in the area where the new village was built. They are now gone. The lintel of a door of the smiddy bore the date 1795.

After some applications had been made to him for feus at Newtyle, Andrew Dalgairns of Ingliston (factor to the estate), in 1828, advised Lord Wharncliffe not to grant new leases on farms near the proposed railway terminus. He suggested rather to give them annual leases as he predicted that the feus could rise to an annual rent of £25 per acre [117]. He then asked permission to advertise for a plan for a new village at Newtyle offering ten guineas for the best by February 20, 1832. Six plans were entered. Lord Wharncliffe preferred the one drawn by George Mathewson, Dundee. The draft of the leases was made out by Christopher Kerr, Dundee, the estate's law agent.

So the new village was deliberately planned and the streets made, and even named, before any house was built. Between 1832 and 1838, £1,053 was spent on plans, roads, water supply and drainage.

According to the *New Statistical Account* of 1842 'the streets in this village have been formed on the principle recommended by the late Sir H. Parnell, by putting the lower stratum of metal on end, breaking the tops to a uniform height, and over-laying with broken metal in the ordinary manner.'

The landowner was always keen to have houses built on his land as this increased its value. James Mackenzie was no exception. There would be a further increase in value if the village could incorporate some industry, such as flax or quarrying, to retain enough of a 'working force' to warrant building small houses close together. There would also be a number of lower middle-class houses for shop-keepers, etc., and the odd professional—teacher, manager, doctor, retired ladies, etc. Add to that, larger houses for those who could afford to commute to work at a distance.

We also find Mr Nairne of Drumkilbo in 1838 [121] advertising plots to let at Kirkinch to form a manufacturing village, and in 1836 George Kinloch planning a residential village at Ardler, naming it Washington after George's hero. There were also in 1897 and in 1913 plans for expanding Newtyle into a residential community. None of these came off, but—they were all based on the railway as a focal point.

The new village of Newtyle *did* come off. In 1833 an advertisement in the *Dundee, Perth and Cupar Advertiser* stated that there would be a public roup on 30th September of ground on leases of 99 years, emphasising 'part of the Belmont Estate in which the Newtyle depots at the termination of the Railway are situated, to be laid out for a Village, according to a plan by Mr Mathewson, architect.' Fifty-one lots were sold that day.

The continuation of the sale was advertised in the same paper for 4th October 1833:

'At the Roup on Monday 30th September, every lot offered for sale, being in all 51 lots, containing nearly 8 acres, and comprising the whole East Half of the Village, were disposed of: and the Roup was then Adjourned until Monday the 28th October .... at twelve o'clock.'

The rest were west of Castle Street, and between it and the turnpike road. The advertisement goes on to say:

'There can now be no doubt that this Village will immediately become a place of considerable importance. It is the wish of the Proprietor to encourage industrious persons: and therefore the same liberal terms which were offered the first day, and gave such general satisfaction will be continued at the Adjourned Sale. Afterwards, if any of the lots remain, the price will most likely be increased.'

Despite all the glorious encouragement only seventeen lots were sold. Another public roup was advertised for Tuesday 19th May 1835 at 12 o'clock. But only two of the remaining 30 lots each of 24 poles, were sold. One paragraph in this advertisement is worth repeating:

'The public are already aware of the great advantages which this village enjoys. Stones and other materials are got at extremely low rates. The Dundee Railway terminates in the Village, and the Coupar Angus and Glammis Railways (both of which are now about to be begun) terminate at the same place: so this Village will be the centre at which the three Railways will unite. Public wells are erected giving ample supply of water. The streets are all formed. The linen manufacture is already begun: and there is strong reason to expect that, in a very short time, waterfalls will be brought into operation, introducing spinning machinery and bleachfields. In short there are few places which promise to rise so rapidly as this Village: and those investing money in building may look for a sure return, and within a short time, a great rise in value.'

Behind the glossy blurb is a brief survey of the village and its hopes at that time.

The advertisements for houses about that time were directed at weavers. Examples were:

(1) 30 October 1835. 'To WEAVERS, To let, at Newtyle. A number of DWELLING HOUSES and WEAVING SHOPS' (there is no clue as to where these were).

(2) 3 March 1837. 'SEVERAL HOUSES and GARDENS . . . to let. Weavers preferred. Apply to George Moon, manufacturer, Newtyle.'

(George Moon had a 32-loom factory and warehouse in what is locally known as the 'Jam Factory.' He also built 16 houses in Belmont Street. It could be some of these houses advertised).

(3) 18 May 1838. A cottage of 5 apartments with attics, garden, etc., advertised at a rent of £11 a year; also 'A number of LOW HOUSES capable of holding four looms each. Very suitable for weavers or others. Rents— £2 each.'

(4) 2 August 1839.

 (a) 'Cottage of one story and attics with garden, at presently occupied by Mr Alison.'

 (This is No. 29 North Street).

 (b) 'Large tenement of two stories—five weaving shops on the ground floor, each with four loom-stances, and five two-roomed houses above.'

 (These are now two houses—Nos. 27 and 25 North Street).

 (c) '. . . tenement of two stories—weaving-shop and dwelling-house.'
 (This would be No. 23 North Street, now demolished) [121].

On 8 July, 1836, 4 new cottages were advertised as being 'opposite the landing-place of the Railway.' These would be Nos. 4, 6, 8, and 10 Commercial Street [121].

There seems to have been some rivalry about who would have the first 'reekin lum' in the new village. John Jack's father came from Blairgowrie to live in Church Street in 1832, and lays claim to this honour [30], but so does the builder of 'Croftness' 46 Belmont Street. As someone has said—it is possible to have a 'reekin lum' without having the roof on: so let us say that these were the first two houses to be built in the new village.

Newtyle—place by place

Auchtertyre (for early history see page 3)

The name seems to come from the Gaelic—*Uachdair tir*—meaning the 'head or upper part of the good land.'

The Duke of Montrose's army camped in a field here when he was thinking of attacking Lord Lindsay in Hatton Castle. It is known as 'Camp Field.' The *New Statistical Account* of 1842 suggests that it may have been the Earl of Crawford, but it was more likely to be Montrose.

A well called the Crewe Well stands near the earth works in Camp Field, and in the north-west of the parish are Grahame's* Knowe and King's Well, the latter marking, it is said, the route taken by Macbeth northwards from his fortress on Dunsinane Hill.

Hugh Watson, of Aberdeen-Angus cattle fame, farmed both Keillor and Auchtertyre. His name is attached to an advertisement in the *Dundee, Perth and Cupar Advertiser* of 3 March 1837, for letting of the house at Auchtertyre. In it is noted 'within ten minutes walk of the Depots of The Dundee, Coupar Angus and Glammis Railways at Newtyle. A cow's keep and other conveniences may be added.'

Balcraig Castle

Baille Craig means 'toun of a rock at the foot of a hill.'

No trace of this remains, beyond being marked on the Ordnance Survey maps. The *Imperial Gazatteer* of 1871 [42] calls it Balcraid, but this could be a misprint. The *Ordnance Gazatteer* of 1903 [39] calls it a 'quondam, castle, but as that means 'former' castle, this is no help. The *New Statistical Account* of 1842 says 'About its site, some urns in a broken state were turned up by the plough not many years ago.' So we are left with the possibility of an old castle or fortified earthwork.

Balmaw or Balmain [113]

The origin of the word *Balmaw* is Gaelic meaning 'a good toun.'

This was gifted to the Abbey of Lindores by King Alexander III on 12 November 1247, and confirmed by King David II on 20 September 1365. About 1480 this entry is in the Abbey books:

> 'Balman fewit for XV lib.
> xij geis, xxxvj powtre
> with the harrag and carrage.'

In 1542 the Abbot of Lindores granted charter to Janet, widow of Archibald Anderson of Bournemouth, and her brother George Blair, the lands of Balmaw or Balmain, Newtyle. In return, as well as money, they were to provide sufficient carriages for conveying the Abbot's goods bought in the market of Cupar in Angus, to the water of the Tay near Lindores. They were also to ride with the Abbot's men in the army of the king, or sufficient horse to bear the Abbot's carriages, against invaders of the realm in time of war. They also had to give lodgings to the Abbot's servants—'all as they

*Marquis of Montrose.

were wont to do.' In other words, Archibald Anderson died without heir, and the land was transferred to his widow and brother, and everything was to go on as usual.

Balmaw came into the hands of the Bannatynes and from them to a family named Gray in 1643. Fifty years later it passed to George Brown of Lidgertlaw, and finally it became part of the estate of James Mackenzie of Belmont.

When the railway was extended northwards about 1860 Balmaw was in the path of the new line to Coupar Angus and Glamis, so it was probably incorporated into Burnmouth farm.

Bannatyne House
> 'For men of law, I wait not quhair to luke
> James Bannatyne was anis a man of skill.'

In 1180 King William the Lyon granted a charter of the kirklands of Newtyld to the newly founded Abbey of Arbroath. In the early 13th century these lands were held by Neil, 2nd Earl of Carrick, grandfather of Robert the Bruce; and not long after that by the Comyn Earls of Buchan [113].

The name Bannatyne seems to have had a number of different spellings, viz—Ballantine and Bellenden—their common ancestor being Nicholas de Benothyn, chancellor to King William about 1180.

The first Bannatyne connected with Newtyle was John. In 1540 he was appointed by the king as curator to the Laird of Glamis during his minority. By 1551 he was designated 'of Newtyle' and was in possession of the kirklands. Being Laird of Newtyle he must have had a house or keep there in 1550 or even earlier.

John's son, James, succeeded to these lands in 1560 and we find records of a contract between James and the Earl of Rothes dated 1577, mentioning the 'new slate house built by James.'

James had a numerous family by his second wife, Katherine Tailliefer· She is recorded by one of her sons, the famous George, to have been 'a woman of godly conversation with whom her husband led a godly, christian and pleasant life. Their children were twenty-three in number. [11].

Their son, George, is best known because it was he who, in 1567, while staying at Bannatyne for about three months, wrote out the unique collection of Scots vernacular verse, known as the *Bannatyne Manuscripts*, now in the Scottish National Library, Edinburgh. He had been collecting them since about 1560, and when the plague raged in Edinburgh, he came to Newtyle. At 23 years of age he carried out the mammoth task of writing out these manuscripts. The poems include those of Henryson, Dunbar, Sir David Lindsay, Alexander Scott, John Bellenden (George's uncle).

James died in 1583 and his son Thomas (brother of George) was 'retoured in the lands of Newtyle with the brewhouse and tiend corn, and half the barony of Balmain' [113]. Thomas, Lord Newtyle, died in 1591 and was succeeded by his younger brother, James; who in turn died in 1597 and was succeeded by his son, also named James. In 1626 James was elevated to the bench as Lord of Sessions. His second wife was Sybella Cockburn, daugher of Lord Cockburn of Newhall, and when he died in 1636 Newhall in Midlothian became the seat of this branch of the family.

The barony of Newtyle, in 1627, passed by purchase to William Hally-burton of Pitcur—except Bannatyne. But when Margaret Hallyburton married Sir George Mackenzie in 1660 Bannatyne and the kirklands became part of her dowry. (This George Mackenzie was none other than the judge, Bloody Mackenzie, the terror of the Covenanters. He also founded the National Library of Scotland in 1689). By this marriage there was a son, George, who succeeded to Bannatyne in 1691.

This George was a Jacobite and was fighting for James Stuart, the Old Pretender, in 1715. George died without issue and the estate passed to the Earl of Bute who left it to his second son, James Stuart. He assumed the name Mackenzie to get the property of Rosehaugh in the Black Isle.

James Stuart Mackenzie did not stay in Bannatyne for long because in 1752 he disentailed the Rosehaugh estate, and bought Kirkhill near Meigle. There he built Belmont Castle, and in 1761 the Hon. James Stuart Mackenzie was appointed Lord Privy Seal.

Towards the end of the 18th century Bannatyne House was much reduced in size, more suitable for the residence of the factor. In so doing the work of John Mylne, master mason to the Crown of Scotland, in extending the house in 1589, was demolished.

The house was occupied by the Watson family who were factors to the Belmont estate. Hugh Watson was born there in 1789. Later he farmed Keillor, Auchtertyre and Bannatyne Home farms, and established the Aberdeen-Angus breed of cattle.

In 1872 Belmont estate [116] was put on the market but not sold. The following is an abbreviated description of Bannatyne House from the sale catalogue:

'within 5 minutes walk of Newtyle Railway Station: built of stone, stuccoed and finished with two turrets: approached from the high road by a carriage drive, bordered by shrubs and evergreens.

Ground floor—entrance hall; dining-room 26ft x 16ft; smoking-room; kitchen; pantry; scullery; wine cellar and water closet.

First floor—a good drawing-room 26ft x 16ft; bath room with hot and cold water supply; 3 bed-rooms and nursery; and water closet.

Second floor—3 attic chambers and turret closets. The house is supplied with water from a self-supplying cistern; and gas is laid on to the top story.

Outbuildings and offices—laundry; two coach houses; two loose-boxes with rooms over; small byre; fodder houses and dog kennel.'

In 1887 the Wharncliffe trustees sold the house of Bannatyne to Alexander H. Moncur, ex-Lord Provost of Dundee. He enlarged the house to make it into a holiday home for working women from Dundee's jute mills. (It was from jute that Moncur made his fortune).

On 21 July 1942 an open-air concert was held at Bannatyne Home of Rest to celebrate its jubilee, having been officially gifted and endowed on 21 July 1892. By 1961 the Home was in difficulties. It had been able to provide for 50 people, giving them a week's holiday plus bus ticket for 25/-. It was running at a loss of about £2,000 per year and subscribers were more difficult to find—so it closed.

There were suggestions that the house become some kind of institution, possibly an open prison, but in 1962 it was sold to Col. James Bannatyne.

In 1865 Major Thomas, who rented Bannatyne House from the Wharncliffe Estates, presented a piece of stone carving to the Society of Antiquaries of Scotland. This was a 'block of grey sandstone, about 12in x 8in and 6in thick. On one side is sculptured in high relief a portion of a human figure, with a flowing robe from the waist downwards: it shows also portion of an arm and a necklace, or chain, with pendant. It was found when taking down some old walls at Bannatyne or Ballantyne House, Newtyle, Forfarshire' [8].

Hatton or Newtyle Castle

This castle was probably built on or near the site of an earlier building, because we find Robert the Bruce signing a charter about 1320 at the 'Haltoun of Newtyld' [113].

Lawrence, 4th Lord Oliphant, built the Castle of Newtyle in 1575. He died in Caithness in 1593 and was buried at Wick.

Hatton must be a derivative of 'Hall Toun,' the farm or house near the Hall or Manor. To be correct the farm is Hatton and the Castle that of Newtyle, but generations of usage have caused the castle to be called Hatton also. There is a stone set in one of the steadings. It must have come from somewhere else and had been built into the wall. It is more elaborate than the usual mason's mark and date. There are a few possibilities—from an old mill (hearsay); or from a castle, or chapel either separate or attached to the castle.

Hatton or Newtyle Castle

From the Register of the Privy Council of Scotland, Vol. VI, 1599-1604. Page 3—1599:

> 'To denounce David Gray and others for not appearing to a charge of deforcement of a herald.
>
> 'Complaint by Laurence, Lord Oliphant, Williame, Earl of Morton, Johnne, Earl of Mar, Alexander, Lord Home and Williame Oliphant of Gask, tutors and curator to the said Lord Oliphant, for their interest as follows—Upon 31st March last, David Gray, son of Gray of Scheilhill, Thomas McGibbun, Servitor to Johnne, Master of Oliphant, Williame Millar, also his servant, Williame Flouris in Drumkilbo, Hew Hammiltoun, Servant to Captain Gray, brother of Gray of Queith, and Robert Ramsay in Foullis, with convocation of the lieges, all armed with hagbuts and pistolets, came to the said Lord Oliphant's house of Newtyle, violently broke

up the gates thereof, surprised the same, and fortified and kept it a long time 'as ane house of weir.' Whereupon letters had been directed with a herald charging them to render the said house. While the letters were being executed by the said herald 'with his displayit coitt of armes,' the said persons shot hagbuts and pistolets at him furth of the said house, on set purpose to have slain him. They had thus treasonably refused to deliver the said house till they understood that the sheriff of the shire was coming with his whole forces, by his Majesty's direction, to recover it: 'And sua for feir of that persute,' they left the said house—charge had been given to the foresaid defenders (except Hew Hammiltoun and Robert Gray) to appear and answer: and now, none of those charged appearing while the pursuers appear by Andro Kneland, their procurator, the order is to Denohnce the defaulters rebels.'

Hatton Castle narrowly escaped being attacked in 1645-6 [113] then occupied by the Earl of Crawford (Lord Lindsay) and a garrison in the interests of the Covenanters. The Marquis of Montrose was for the royal cause and came from the north to strike a blow at Lindsay. After the Battle of Auldearn he left Badenoch and marched south as far as Newton of Blair. It is said that he camped at Auchtertyre. There the Gordons deserted him and the Highlanders stole off home to their glens with their plunder. Montrose abandoned his attack on Hatton, and contented himself with burning Newton Castle, Blairgowrie, on his way back north.

About 50 years later we find the Bishop of Aberdeen staying at Hatton. There is a note in the Session Records of 8 May 1698, ten years after the revolution, 'which day the presbitry violently entered the church by breaking up the doors thereof: so that from the 8th day of May foresaid, the parishioners did convene to the Haltoun where they are to have sermon maintained by the Bishop Aberdeen and others in his name, during his abode in the parioch.'

The prelacy still had a strong hold in the parish, and we find notices of the Bishop continuing public services at Haltoun right on to at least 1710. The Presbyterian minister did not get possession of the parish books, utensils, etc., until 1719 and only after taking legal action.

In 1715, during the uprising, we find the power of the Jacobites great enough in this area to shut down the church against the Presbyterian minister and they 'violated with their soldiery the sanctity of his house.' There is no indication of Bishop Aberdeen being in Hatton in 1715, nor of when it ceased to be occupied, but it looks as if it were left derelict some time during the first quarter of the 18th century.

It seems that this house was not intended as a fortress although Lord Oliphant is said to have planted a cannon on the battlements. It is certainly well-positioned to guard the glack or pass from Dundee via Auchterhouse, and, of course, invite travellers to rest—probably at a cost.

HATTON CASTLE

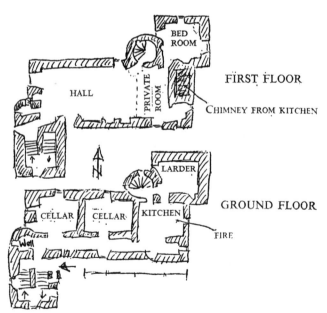

From 'McGibbon & Ross' 1887-92

16

The following description is taken from McGibbon and Ross 1887-1892 [57]:

'A ruinous mansion . . . now forms an adjunct to the garden of the farm-house of Castlemains. It is built on the Z-plan having a square tower at the north-east and south-west angles. The latter contains the entrance doorway, and a square staircase with steps 5ft long, which leads to the first floor level. The ground floor is vaulted, and exhibits the usual arrangements, comprising the kitchen, with its large fireplace and a larder adjoining, and two cellars entering from the passage. All the walls of this floor are well supplied with shot-holes flanking the castle in every direction. A circular turret in the re-entering angle of the north-east tower, leads from the basement to the first floor, and continues up to the upper floors. This stair was evidently the private one to the family apartments, connected as it is with the private room and the kitchen. There are indications of another stair turret having been carried up in the angle of the south-west tower. This was almost certainly the case, but there have been alterations and repairs made at this part of the building, when the stair was probably removed. The first floor contains the hall, which is 35 feet by 18 feet, with the usual private room adjoining, from which a bedroom opens in the north-east wing. In the upper floors there seems, from the levels of the windows, to have been an extra number of stories introduced over the private room and the bedroom in the North-east wing. The upper floors are all lighted with large windows. The gables were no doubt finished with crow-steps, and the dormers with enriched gablets, but the few ornamental features which the building may have had once possessed have been destroyed, and little of interest now remains except the plan.'

The Oliphants were a widespread family, and although their crests vary, all of them have three crescents. The Newtyle one in addition had a unicorn's head with foliage behind it; and the motto *A tout pouvyre a tout povoire* with two elephants as supporters. The motto is old French and could well mean—'Where there's a will there's a way.'

A bronze socketed axe-head, dated about 500 B.C. was found at Hatton in 1910 [7].

Keillor [113] (for the Keillor stone see page 4)

Near Hill of Keillor there is a field called Chesterpark from the Latin *castra* indicating a Roman post or station. It lies on the high ground east of the standing stone.

In 1296 Randolph de Kelore did homage to King Edward, and was probably a vassal of the Earl of Strathmore. The homage was paid at two different times in 1296—first at the castle of Kildrummie (Aberdeenshire) and secondly at Berwick-on-Tweed. In 1384 John de Kelor, the last of the family to hold lands in Angus, parted with his estate to John of Ardillar (or Ardler) for an annual of six merks out of the two touns of Keillor. Then Easter Keillor passed into the hands of the Harkers and the Ogilvys until 1645 when it fell to Susan Haldane from Gleneagles.

Tradition has it that King James while travelling incognito was shown some kindness by the 'auld guidwives,' so he increased the estate on condition:

> 'Ye Haddens o' the Moor, ye pay nocht
> But a hairen tither, if it's socht,
> A red rose at Yule, and a sna' ba' at Lammas.'

A hairen tither is a rope made of hair. There is grave doubt about this story, and it could just as well have been about the Haddens who held land near Alyth.

On 8 January 1648 James Hallyburton of Keillor fell heir to Wester Keillor, when his father, George, was killed at the Battle of Tippermuir. Along with Wester Keillor went the mill and pendicle of Hill of Keillor and Denside.

On 29 October 1695 John, Earl of Strathmore and Kinghorne, came into possession of the lands of Keillor. Robert III gave Walter Ogilvy a charter of the lands of Easter Keillor, and these lands stayed in the hands of the Ogilvys for some time [113 and 43]. Then it passed into the hands of the Earl of Wharncliffe.

The *New Statistical Account* of 1842 [101] calls Hill of Keillor a village, and the *Imperial Gazetteer* of 1871 calls the Chapel of Keillor a village. This sounds an exaggeration, but no doubt there were more houses than there are now. 'Keillaird' or 'Kill-aird' means a church or burial-place on an eminence.

Kinpurney Tower and Privy's Prap

There are various spellings—Kilpurnie: Kinpurnie: Kilpirnie: Kinpirnie: Kynprony. The name seems to derive from the Gaelic *kin-fuarin* or *ceann buerne* meaning 'the head of the small streams.'

The hill is 1,134 feet above sea level and was used as a station for signal fires. It is said that there was a fort of pre-Roman age similar to that on Denoon Hill [62]. If so, it was probably an earth fort.

James Mackenzie of Belmont Castle built both the tower and the prap in 1774. The tower is approximately 30 feet by 20 feet and 40 feet high, with two doorways facing south; window openings on the other sides and blind windows above. The walls are three feet thick. In its original design the east, north and west walls were battlemented, and the south wall was much lower without battlements. There was a lean-to slate roof, and inside a fireplace; an alcove 'cupboard,' and a wooden floor.

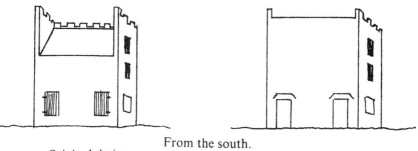

From the south.

Original design.   Later design.

Not long after it was built the roof was removed (or collapsed). The Belmont Sale Catalogue of 1872 [116] notes 'the dismantled tower on Kinpurnie Hill.' The front or south wall was carried up to the parapet, probably to protect the side walls from high winds, and the top left without battlements. The doorways were also changed, and for years allowed cattle and sheep to enter for shelter.

James Playfair, minister of Newtyle from 1770-7 became involved in Mackenzie's work, and it has been said that Playfair or his son was the architect of the tower. True or not, while James Mackenzie was at Belmont, Playfair was a constant companion. Mackenzie had him transferred to Meigle, probably to have him nearer. Many authors claim that these two used the tower as an observatory, and 'spent many a night there studying the stars'—and the nights could be bitterly cold and windy. A keeper's cottage was supposed to have been built near the tower—but no records of this have been found. One wonders who would live up there—water, food and firewood would all have to be carried up.

Mackenzie may have originally intended to use the tower as an observatory, but there is no indication that he ever did. But he *did* build an observatory at Belmont Castle. It was designed by the Rev. Alexander Bryce, who also gave Mackenzie a 'sophisticated' sundial. He installed a few Dolland and Ramsden telescopes, and set up a Sisson large equatorial telescope on a pillar. Weather records were kept at Belmont from 1782 to 1797 [20 and 37].

Mackenzie also set up a meridian mark on the lawn at Belmont. It was shaped like this ⟂. With his prap on the skyline as another meridian, he was able to check his clocks fairly accurately.

All through his notes James Mackenzie refers to the tower as Banquo's Tower. (This name is also used in *Black's Tourist of Scotland* of 1852 [14].) He used it with the prap and a base line at Belmont as triangulation points to estimate heights and distances of hills and mountains (see inside back cover). He also used the method of fall in atmospheric pressure with height (i.e. the barometer/altimeter) to measure the Sidlaws [20 and 37]. There are unfortunately a number of errors in his calculations.

According to James's own measurements the observatory at Belmont was located at 56° 35' 0" N : 3° 11' 15" W.

From about 1840 Kinpurney tower has remained derelict and roofless. We find Guthrie [40] recommending that it be repaired as far back as 1875. It is a well-known landmark, but—a 'Castle Folley' [61].

In 1972 the tower was in such a condition that it either had to come down or be repaired. Because it was a landmark, repairs were carried out at a cost of approximately £6,000 shared by Angus County Council and the Cayzer estate. The estate took on the arduous task of cartage up the hill by Land Rover and tractor, of materials and equipment. The work was done in July and August 1974.

There is a tale about David Gray the hermit of Kinpurney Hill [52]. One version was printed in the *Kirriemuir Free Press* in 1918 and reprinted in September 1953. This claimed that Davy stayed there for seven years.

The other version was re-told by Colin Gibson in the *Dundee Courier* of 28 March 1970, that Davy stayed for a year (or a year and a day) for a wager. These tales which are passed down are difficult to assess. Because Davy was a poacher, it would be worth a pound or two from the landlords to pay the wager just to keep him off the land for a year. Also, being a poacher, Davy would not starve, even on the top of Kinpurney Hill.

The view from the top has been noted, often lyrically, by quite a number of authors, leaving one wondering if they had ever been to the top at all. Many repeat what their predecessors have said—'on a clear day anyone with keen eyesight can pick out St Abb's Head to the south and Lochnagar to the north' [44]. Or 'the Tay on its course—the rich vale of the Carse—the estuary of the Tay—St Andrews and its venerable towers— . . . the Bell Rock lighthouse in the German Ocean—the hill and turret form, it is said, a useful landmark for vessels at sea' [101, 1842]. Without being too poetical about it, most hill-walkers will agree that the tower has made interesting one of the least interesting hills of the Sidlaws.

'Privy's Prap' or 'Preerie's Prap,' or however it is spelt, simply means the 'prop' built by the 'Privy' Councillor. It is a solid stone pillar about 20 feet high supporting a stone ball, and it stands on Keillor Hill. It is on the meridian of Belmont Castle, i.e. dead south [91].

Kinpurnie Castle [130].

Sir Charles Cayzer of Gartmore, Stirlingshire, bought 4,300 acres of the Newtyle estate from the Wharncliffe Trustees in 1902. He commissioned Thomas Wilkie, architect, Dundee, to build the mansion house as well as other houses in Newtyle, and Burnmouth farm house. Kinpurnie Castle was built in 1907-8 on a site on the north side of Keillor Hill—a site with an extensive view of Strathmore. The front porch at the west end was added in 1910. It is now the home of Sir James Cayzer and his mother, Lady Cayzer.

Kirkinch

Inch meaning 'island' is common enough all over Scotland, but this island has a church (now in ruins) on it—so Kirkinch got its name. This country round Kirkinch was part of the Devonian sea, which deteriorated over millions of years to become bog and marsh by the 18th century. The bog was bad enough by 1800 for the whisky smugglers to dodge the gougers or excisemen. Instead of coming round by Meigle where the gougers could be waiting, the smugglers could take the risky short-cut through the bog which they knew and the gougers did not. Kirkinch to Hatton of Newtyle was one leg of a whisky trail from Speyside to Dundee [100—1975].

About 1823 a long straight 'muckle ditch' was dug between Kirkinch and Drumkilbo to drain the bog by running the water into the River Dean [100—1974]. By the end of the century this ditch had reduced to a mere trickle of brackish water, but it had served its purpose. A similar bog at Ardler had been cleared about 1760 [115].

The church was erected in 1695, and in the autumn of 1830, during the ministry of the Rev. Mr. Floridew, the roof fell in. The story goes that the minister had announced that it had been 'a bad, bad harvest.' He advised his flock to take advantage of the better weather, and return to the fields that Sunday rather than stay in church. He had no sooner finished his statement, when the roof fell in!!

Kirkinch was one of the halts on the Newtyle to Glamis Railway. Mr Nairne of Drumkilbo tried to plan a new manufacturing village at Kirkinch, similar to that at Newtyle. He advertised in the *Dundee Advertiser* of 30 March, 1838, that he was feuing ground at Kirkinch to form this village. One of the incentives to buy a plot of ground was that houses of £10 yearly value would give the necessary qualifications for a vote in the county. Also, as the village straddled the border, the buyer had the choice of a vote either in the Counties of Angus or Perth—or in both!! This plan was soon abandoned.

The main Perth to Aberdeen line ran close by, and eventually level-crossing gates were put up. From 1918 it was manned by Mrs Mary Stewart for 30 years, then by her daughter, Mrs Phemie Forbes, until 15 July 1968, when the crossing ceased to be operated.

The villagers carried their water from the Cally well for drinking and cooking—washing water came from rain water collected in barrels from the roof. The name 'Cally' could have derived from 'chalybite'—an iron ore. So the water would permeate through the ore carrying dissolved iron salts and some insoluble particles, making hard but good drinking water. The elder inhabitants of Kirkinch used to attribute their long life to drinking this water.

Mundamalla House

It was built about 1886 at the junction of the Newtyle-Meigle and the Newtyle-Kettins roads. It was occupied by Robert Sim, a retired jute merchant from India. He died in 1912, when the house was occupied by his son, William K. Sim. The Sims also bought West Cottage in the Kettins Road as a house for gardener, coachman or chauffeur, at various times.

It was eventually sold in 1937 to become a holiday home for the outdoor blind. At that time it had 3 public rooms; 5 bedrooms; bathroom; 2 servants' bedrooms; laundry; washing house; coal cellar; large garage; central heating and electric light. It was set in two acres of ground and assessed at £92. 'A low price will be accepted.' (*Dundee Courier*, 9 April 1937).

Newbigging

This is the name of many localities in Scotland, varying in size from a single farm to large villages. It seems to be a corruption of 'new building.' Macpherson in 1885 [61] gives Newtibber as its original name—*tobar* meaning 'well.' There were quite a number of wells, e.g. Doggie's well (a spring with a low outlet); Coffin well (from its shape); Stevenson's well (in front of his house—dug down). The reasonable ease with which water could be obtained all the year round, could be one of the reasons for the origin of this settlement.

Newbigging existed long before the new village of Newtyle was built (1832). It had a population of about 230 when Newtyle was only a small farm toun. Newbigging started to decline after Newtyle became a village and the railway built:

1842—population 229; 60 houses; 32 pendicles
1871—   ,,   160; c40   ,, ; 15 ,,
1901—   ,,   c50; 13   ,, ;   3 ,,
(the number of houses includes the pendicles).

The pendicles were gradually swallowed up by Auchtertyre, Newbigging and Ralston farms.

A list of crofters in the early 1850s is interesting, if only because some were known by nicknames—probably no one knew their names anyway:

The Grays (builders)	Treaclie
Mrs Stevenson	Jock Taylor
Solomon	Sandy Moon
John Stewart, Etherty	The Calleries
Taylor Robertson	James Ireland
Sandy Grewar	Jeffery
Pate Lyon	Robbie Guild
Patie Martin	Robert Chaplin
Geordie Robertson (best coo in Newbigging)	
Adam Gley Argyle	Johnnie Anderson
Bob Ireland	Geordie Deuchars
G. Tosh	The Wingle
Peter Anderson (back of toll)	Crockett (toll-keeper)

(I am indebted to the late Rose Jeffery, postmistress, for keeping her mother's list).

Chapter 2

THE CHURCH

The history of the church in Newtyle is obscure in its early years. There was a chapel in the parish of Keillor, and a Well of St Bride at Templeton. There is some memory of carved stones at the Chapel of Keillor smiddy, but none have been found.

The earliest record is when the Church of 'Nevtyl' in the diocese of St Andrews was dedicated by Bishop David in 1242. It was later given by William the Lion to the Abbey of Arbroath. Sir Andrew Lindsay became vicar in 1566 (Feu Charter of Kirklands) and in 1567 John Nevay had Nevay and Eassie in his charge as well as Newtyle. He was transferred to Glamis about 1571 [113].

Maister Robert Boyd, minister of Glamis about 1567, was presented to the vicarage of Newtyle and Nevay by James VI on 5 July 1571. He had a stipend of £80 Scots and the kirklands. One incident happened during his forty years or so in Newtyle:

> 'In the Assembly of October 1577, John Anderson compeared in linen clothes and prostrate on his knees, confessing he had offended Maister Boyd by drawing his blood. Whereof he repented and asked for forgiveness, promising by the grace of God not to fall into like wickedness' [95].

Boyd died in 1610.

He was followed by George Patullo (primus), and he, in turn, by his son George Patullo (secondus) in 1647. The second George was transferred to Kingsbarns in 1663. Andrew Bruce was the next minister. He died in December 1669 aged about 33.

His successor, Thomas Black, in 1670, was 'constrained to relinquish his charge' at Newtyle and his licence taken from him. He was denounced in 1684 for not keeping the anniversary of the Reformation, and for not appearing before the Council when cited [95].

One minister, Alexander Mackenzie from 1685 to 1698, was a relative of Sir George Mackenzie, Lord Advocate and the Bloody Mackenzie*. Alexander was summoned before the Privy Council on 3 October 1689, for not reading the Proclamation of the Estates, and for not praying for William and Mary. He was acquitted but deprived of his charge on 5 December 1695. But, backed by the Bishop of Aberdeen, then residing in Hatton Castle, he continued episcopalian services in a meeting-house with quite a large following. During the Rebellion of 1715 he took possession of the church, and conducted services there. He removed to Edinburgh, where he died in 1722 aged about 58 [95].

*Laird of Newtyle, see page 13.

23

The Parish Church. Built 1767. Destroyed 1867.

The Parish Church. Built 1872.

The minister apponted in his place in 1689 was George Clephane. He found that there were so many attending the episcopalian church services and so few attending his own services that he was unable to form a kirk session. He continued to pray for King George, and during the uprising of 1715 held services in the manse while Mackenzie occupied the church. The Jacobites threatened to take him prisoner and bring him before the Governor of Perth. He was arrested in the manse by a number of armed men who 'removed a considerable part of his goods, frightened his wife and children, broke open locked doors, and even stabbed the beds with naked swords' [95]. He did succeed in getting the support of his parishioners and recover the communion cups taken by Mackenzie. George Clephane died on 27 January 1730 aged about 66, and was succeeded by his son, Thomas. Thomas's term of office was uneventful. He had two daughters and seven sons.

In 1770 James Playfair, father of the distinguished architect William Playfair, was presented by the Hon. James Stuart Mackenzie of Belmont Castle. The previous minister, Thomas Clephane, was presented by Ann, Countess of Bute, who owned the Newtyle area. Now James Playfair and others for about 70 years, depended on the patronage of the landlord for their living. He became involved in Mackenzie's astronomical and mathematical ideas and took some part in the building of 'Preerie's prap' and the tower on Kinpurnie Hill. He was transferred to Meigle on 10 October, 1777, probably to be nearer the laird. Later he was to become Professor of Theology at the Sorbonne University, Paris.

He was succeeded in 1778 at Newtyle by the Rev. Alexander Small who wrote the account of Newtyle parish in the *Statistical Account of Scotland* for 1792. He was transferred to Kilconquhar on 10 November, 1791.

The next three ministers seemed to have had uneventful service— Thomas Barty in 1792; John MacPherson Cunningham in 1815; and Robert Smith in 1818.

John Moon, born in 1790, was presented to Newtyle Church in 1825. He was the son of John Moon, farmer and linen manufacturer of New-bigging and Newtyle. John (junior) had seven daughters and three sons, and wrote the account of the parish of Newtyle in the *New Statistical Account* of 1842. He died on 20 November, 1862.

Then came John Chalmers in 1863 followed by George Brown in 1871. The minister from 1874 to 1918 was George Bell Lunan, a distinguished linguist, a botanist, and 'a model parish minister much respected by his brethren and by his parishioners' [95].

During the last half of the 18th century there was some dissatisfaction with the government of the established or parish church, causing a number of break-away movements. There was no effect on Newtyle until the new village was built. One of these 'rebel' movements was the Secession or Presbyterian Church (later the United Presbyterian or U.P. church).

The congregation was contemporary with the village and until a church was built they met for worship in one of the lofts of the bone mill. Also for a time they met in the old railway depot—a place possessing only side walls and a roof. The church was built in 1835. The first sermon was preached on the 2 August although 'it was without floor, seats or pulpit' (*Dundee*

Advertiser, 31 January 1880). It was officially opened on 23 October by Mr Marshall of Lochee.

The Rev. John Muir from Ayrshire was ordained on 6 February 1838. At the soiree held on that occasion the Rev. George Gilfillan of Dundee cracked a joke—'that the people were to be pitied if to a *waning Moon* they had now added a *dreary Muir*' (Rev. John Moon was parish minister at that time).

By the end of 1838 there was a membership of 80 and an attendance of about 200. In 1864 the manse was built next door in Church Street at a cost of £800. Due to ill-health in October 1871 Mr Muir asked to be relieved of his duties. This was agreed, but he was asked to retain his status as minister and given life tenancy of the manse. He died in 1874 and his friend and colleague, the Rev. George Gilfillan from Dundee, preached the funeral sermon.

The congregation was neither large enough nor did it have enough money to provide a new pastor. The Dundee Presbytery continued to supply probationers, and later, students. The church gradually deteriorated until the congregation was down to about 20 by the time of Mr Muir's death. The elders asked that the church be closed down, as they could no longer pay their share of the salary. With a sermon by the Rev. John Dunlop of Alyth the church closed on 1 February, 1880. It was bought by David Clark Burman, and eventually became the village hall—known as the Wharncliffe Hall.

The Free Church [35 and 72]

In 1842 two Dundee ministers, one of whom was Robert Murray McCheyne, began religious meetings in various places in Newtyle until a church was built and opened in 1844 (now the Legion Hall). There were some attempts to unite Meigle and Newtyle as one charge. This never happened but it did delay the sanctioning of Newtyle as a separate charge until 1862. The manse was built in 1871 ('Wardenlea,' Church Street). From the proceeds (£600) of a bazaar held in the Kinnaird Hall, Bank Street, Dundee, in March, 1900, a new church was erected. This became known as the East Church, and later, after the merger in 1938, became the church hall.

The ministers were:

1863   John Fleming . . . died 1904.

1896   Edward Millar—went to Cleveland, Transvaal.

1903   William Maxwell—went to Chalmers Church, Dundee.

1923   John Mechie—he came from New Cumnock Bank Church, where he had been since 1896. He took an active part in the community life of the village, and was very popular.

John Mechie died on 20 February 1938, and then the church and manse were united with the parish church on 4 September 1938. The East Church became the church hall and the manse was sold.

The Rev. Robert Wood came from Patna in Ayrshire, where he had been minister for two years, to take charge of Newtyle on 16 May 1919. He died on 26 June 1949, and was followed by George H. H. McBride in 1950; R. M. Cullen in 1957; John A. Sherrard in 1961; and Robert C. M. Carmichael in 1965.

26

The site of the present parish church must have held a number of churches. There is a stone lintel in the session house dated 1689, and the bell is dated 1736.

The old church was built in 1767 and the manse and offices in 1771. The minister's living [101—1792] including the glebe of six Scots acres, was valued at £80 to £100 Scots. He was paid mainly in victuals—two-thirds meal and one-third barley.

The *New Statistical Account* of 1842 [101] gives the stipend as:

'77 bolls, 1 peck. 4/5s lippie of barley.

75 bolls, 1 firlot, 1 peck, 3/5s lippie of meal.

1 peck, 1/5 lippie of oats,

and L32 11s 5d & 1/12th penny sterling of money.'

The church held about 500 sitters—a few of which were reserved for the poor, and about 100 seats let for a small amount annually on behalf of the poor.

There is some doubt about the fate of this church. Joiner [44] has it burned down, while others say it was pulled down—in 1867. The present church was built between 1870 and 1872, practically on the same site as the old one. It can hold 800 seated and has a pipe organ, electric heating and lighting. The tower has a clock with two faces—one south and one east.

The architect was Andrew Heiton II of Perth, with quite a number of churches, country houses and railway stations to his credit. Examples of his work nearest to Newtyle are—Alyth Public Hall; Balloch near Alyth; Lands of Loyal; and additions to Bonskeid and Hallyburton houses.

Church Tokens [29 and 47]

There were three of these for Newtyle:

(1) 1819 Obverse 'NEWTYLE KIRK'
    Reverse 'REVD. R. SMITH 1819'

(2) 1827 Obverse 'NEWTYLE KIRK MDCCCXXVII
              L.COR XI 23-29'
    Reverse 'LUKE XXII 19-20 THIS DO IN REMEMBRANCE
              OF ME'
    (Some of these tokens have one or two holes in them for an obscure reason—perhaps table numbers or just strung round the neck).

(3) 1838 Obverse 'ASSO. CON. NEWTYLE 1838'
    Reverse 'THIS DO IN REMEMBRANCE OF ME
              LUKE XXII 19.'

The Kirkyaird

On 30 March 1939 the kirkyaird was closed for burials except for certain named relatives, who might wish to be buried there, or for caskets of cremated ashes of relatives.

There are some very old stones dating back to the 17th century with interesting carvings and epitaphs [128]. For example:

'1771

Here lies the dust of Robert Small
Who when in life was thick and tall
But what's of greater consequence
He was endowed with good sense
O how joyful the day on which
Death's prisoner shall be free
And in triumph's o'er all his foes
His God in mercy see.'

The new cemetery was laid out in the manse glebe close to Kirkton farm.

The Episcopalian Church

Joiner [44] counted 15 members of the Episcopalian church living in Newtyle in 1951, but they would have to go elsewhere to worship. The nearest church was just north of Meigle at the junction of the Alyth road. This church is now demolished but their churchyard remains.

Chapter 3

SOCIAL LIFE

'Coals are the fuel used here. They cost from 4s 6d to 5s per boll in Dundee. There are some peats, of a bad quality, and dearer than coal, used for kindling fires. Roads were kept in tolerable repair by the statute labour till last summer when it was commuted. Now there are turnpikes, of whose utility many are not yet satisfied, though it is hoped thay will be so, when the roads are completed. The general scarcity of 1782-3 was felt here. The kirk session bought meal for the poor, and sold it at a reduced price. Oatmeal sold, in summer 1783, at 1s 3d; pease and bear meal at 11d the peck. The poor in some of the hilly countries, bought coarse flour, and mixed it with bran, of which they made bread. Hence the miserable state of the country may easily be conceived' [101—1792].

In feudal Scotland trade was a right given by royal dispensation to boroughs, in return for some service to the baron and the king. This included the kirktowns of Meigle and Newtyle. By the 18th century more than half the inhabitants of Newtyle were weavers living in pendicles or crofts, with a small piece of land, for which they paid a rent of money and/or kind. The Rev. Small writing the *Statistical Account* of 1792, criticises these people as 'Very industrious' on the one hand, and in the same paragraph 'their situation might be meliorated by greater exertion of industry' [101—1792].

Also 'they are not fond of military life.' Only five in the parish of Newtyle, all weavers, enlisted in the 1745 rebellion and were returned after being captured at Culloden [59]. Considering the poverty, hard work and the minimal of food, they were not fit to fight, so the five who fought for Prince Charlie could have been cooks or camp followers.

There was inflation in the second half of the 18th century. Food and wages increased nearly four times, wages lagging a bit. Workmen were paid by the day including victuals. In the Newtyle area a labourer got 6d per day in winter and 8d in summer; carpenters got 8d and 1s; high-paid masons got 1s 8d in summer if they boarded themselves. A married farm servant could get £15 Scots per year (about 2s per week) with house, croft of land, meal, etc.—not a lot to keep a family.

The *Statistical Account* of 1792 puts forward the idea that although wages were four times what they were in 1750 'yet the servants save no more money now than formerly, owing chiefly to their extravagance in dress.' Food had increased between 200% and 400%. Prices in 1790 were—meat 3d to 4d per pound; chickens 4d each; hens 1s to 1s 4d; butter 8d to 9d per pound; cheese 4s 6d per stone (14 lbs); eggs 4d per dozen. Wheat was £1 Scots to £1 4s; oats 12s to 14s; and barley £1 Scots per boll.

In 1790 there were five poor in Newtyle who received alms monthly, with an additional two or three who got occasional charity. This cost about £14 Scots per year, raised by contributions mainly in church collections.

By 1840 there were about 15 poor receiving between 1s and 2s 6d per week, and more in the case of widows with young families, or orphan children. Some of the poor would receive private donations, but only to 'meritorious persons reluctant to apply for relief' and who 'evinced gratitude for the respect shown to their wants' [101—1842]. The same account also comments that 'there is a laudable disinclination among the people to come upon the poor fund.'

Population

Webster's population figures for 1755 [99] gives the following statistics for Newtyle:

> 2 miles long
> 2 miles broad
> 1 parish
> 1 minister
> No. of Protestants 913
> No. of fighting men 182 & 3/5ths.

The last figure is an example of statistics gone mad, and anyway is doubtful.

From 1755 to 1831 the population of Newtyle parish fell from about 900 to 780, then rose sharply to 1264 by 1841 with the building of the new village. Until 1901 there was a gradual decline, mainly due to the depopulation of Newbigging and the decline of the linen trade. There was then a gradual building up as some industry developed, and commuters began to live in Newtyle, most of them working in Dundee.

Commuting to work from Newtyle seemed to start about 1850 with Dundee jute merchants. Professor McIntosh built Nevay Park in 1902 and travelled to St Andrews via Meigle and Perth. The railway, of course, helped a lot, and made it easier to get away from towns and live in the country. By 1961 about 7% of Newtyle's population worked in Dundee. It may be of interest to note that the population of Newtyle parish in 1961 was practically the same as in 1755.

Most of the people of the parish live in the village—in 1842 56% and in 1942 66%. In 1961 about 20% worked in agriculture. Now the trend is a reduction in the number of farm workers, the end of the bothies and the tied farm house.

After 1945 there was also a tendency for retired farm workers to live in the village—many of them being allocated council houses.

In 1842 about 9·7% of the population of the parish were over 65; in 1951 that figure was 8%, and this rose to 12% by 1967. This increase was helped by the council policy to build houses specially for old folk. For some time it was mooted that Newtyle was becoming an old folks' village.

The *Statistical Account* of 1842 [101] notes that 'in some three years past' there was an average of 24 births and 18 deaths per year. Of the births four were illegitimate, and of the deaths four were young people. Also noted is that 'pregnancy among females in the working classes occasionally precedes marriage.' But there is no indication of what happens in the other 'classes.'

30

It is difficult to assess the 'average' number of deaths. To arrive at any comparison, we find that the number of deaths per year from 1960 ranges from 3 or 4 to about 18.

The Armed Services

The 8th Forfarshire Rifle Volunteers were in existence from about 1874 to at least 1882. The commanding officer in 1874 was Mr Mudie who had a grocer's shop at the corner of Belmont Street and Commercial Street. From 1876 the C.O. was Lieutenant (later Captain) John Jack.

They did their winter training in the school for one hour on two nights per week, and used the rifle range at Kinpurnie farm. Occasionally they joined with the Glamis unit for further exercises and shooting at Glamis. They also held an annual supper and entertainment in the school.

There was a residential instructor in Newtyle from 1874 to 1881—Sergeant O'Shaughnessy, who lived in Commercial Street where the armoury was located. He was asked to drill the boys at school for half an hour before or after school hours on two days a week—but he refused the offer.

The 'Volunteers' were replaced by the 'Territorials.' Quite a number of Newtyle men were in the Territorials at the outbreak of the 1914-18 war, and joined the 5th Black Watch. The war memorial records 21 officers and men who died during that time. The school and the bone mill were used for prisoners-of-war.

During the 1939-45 war Polish troops were stationed in various buildings in Newtyle. They left in September 1941, after a farewell function in the school ('no dancing'). Their padre was accustomed after the Sunday service to walk up the hill and sit at a favourite viewpoint. He was missed one day, and found dead at that point in the Bannatyne plantation. A cross was erected there by his fellow soldiers.

A small unit of about 40 Local Defence Volunteers (later the Home Guard) was formed, as well as Observer Corps, Women's Volunteer Service, Fire Auxiliaries, and Red Cross.

Police

The local police station and house was built in 1870 at 16 Church Street, and was occupied by the village policeman. Exactly 100 years later a new police station and house was built in North Street, and the old one sold. The 'village bobby,' as such has gone. He became a member of a team, firstly under a sergeant at Birkhill, and later under Forfar when the new regions and districts were formed.

Housing

Most of the houses in Newtyle were originally privately built, the ground being feued from the estate. Some houses in Belmont Street, Church Street and North Street were built by local linen manufacturers, and let to weavers.

31

Just after the 1914-18 war the Cayzer estate built some houses on the Dundee Road and in Belmont Street. Later the County Council built some houses in Church Street. But most of the council houses building took place from the end of the 1939-45 war. The scheme to the south of the village started out as 14 houses in South Street, then another 42 were built forming Dunarn Street and Terrace. The whole scheme was to have been extended to the Hatton farm road. That never came off, and the new school was built on this site in 1963.

Except for a small scheme of 16 houses on the site of the old school in North Street, the rest of the council house building has been of a gap-filling nature, averaging about 6 houses each. A total of 88 council houses have been built since 1945.

Six houses and the renovation of a three-storey tenement in North Street, have been built privately.

Water Supply

The original supply in 1832 came from a spring in one of the fields on Hatton farm. It was carried in lead pipes to two street wells. The number of wells was increased, as the village grew, to nine—one in North Street, 3 in Church Street, 3 in Belmont Street, and 2 in South Street. It was piped to some buildings at the owners' expense between 1840 and 1870—the Post Office in Church Street; the U.F. Manse; the police station; the school and schoolhouse; and numbers 18 and 26 South Street. Later other houses had it piped in.

Eventually water was taken from the Dundee water main from Lintrathen Loch, and by about 1969 the Fountainhead supply was cut off. There were three reasons for this—expense of upkeep (the County Council would not finance it); the water was becoming suspect; and few houses were left with the old supply.

The old method was to use springs or dig wells. The ease with which water could be obtained was an important reason for location of such settlements as Newbigging. Farms such as Auchtertyre and Kinpurney had tanks uphill fed by springs.

Sewage

The original sewage at the beginning of the village in 1832 was the street. Ditches were dug along each side of the street in an attempt to drain the rough surface. These ditches were a convenient place to lay the water pipes—which may have been all right until they leaked, with not enough pressure to keep out the drain water.

Each house had its garden, a very necessary adjunct to living. At the foot of the garden away from the house was the privy or dry lavatory. This was usually a small semi-portable shed. A hole was dug, about 3 feet deep and about half the size of the shed. The shed was placed over it. The 'seat' was a plank placed at a convenient height. When full, another hole was dug nearby, using the earth to fill the previous hole and the shed was shifted over it.

By the 1930s a sewage plant was positioned about 200 yards east of the village on the Eassie Road. It consisted of two filter beds and a sludge bed.

The outflow was to the Hatton burn, but this led to some pollution when the number of houses increased. A new system was installed in 1972.

Building to the north of the village is very much inhibited because of sewage difficulties. The gradient is far too slow. A flushing plant would need to replace gravity, meaning a costly technical job that would be uneconomic.

Poverty—background

The Scottish Poor Law of 1579 was established 'for the punishment of the strong and idle beggars, and relief of the poor and impotent.' This, as well as the English Elizabethan Poor Law of 1601, were forced upon the statesmen of the time because after the Reformation the church was no longer equal to the task of the needs of the poor, which it had done up to then. The number of vagrants and the 'idle and disorderly' had increased considerably with the social and economic changes of the 15th and 16th centuries.

Relief was given from voluntary church contributions and the heritors (the land-owners in the parish liable to public burdens). Begging was almost recognised as a legal method of supplementing these doles and the professional beggar was a characteristic figure in the social life. It must also be pointed out that religious dissenters were disqualified from relief from the state church collections, and these dissenters were increasing in number between 1815 and 1840.

The Poor Law Amendment Act (Scotland) of 1845 established poor-houses and local authorities known as Parochial Boards.

Poorhouses in towns varied considerably—but the 'well-regulated' ones were the exception rather than the rule. They usually held a host of children, in constant contact with adult paupers. These children were often badly looked after and had little or no education. The treatment of patients in many of the poorhouse infirmaries and sick wards was a scandal. So was the treatment of idiots, imbeciles and lunatics. There was no uniformity in the granting of outdoor relief—some were generous, others completely inadequate. The law was detested by the poor and a growing burden on the rates.

The Newtyle Parochial Board 1845-1895 [75]

In Newtyle the Parochial Board started on 16 September 1845 with a meeting of the heritors and the church, in the session house. From the heritors were Andrew Whitton of Couston; Patrick Millar of Davidstone; and John Kerr, writer (solicitor) Dundee, representing Lord Wharncliffe. From the church were the Rev. John Moon, and three elders, namely—Hugh Watson (of Aberdeen-Angus fame), John Pirrie, and James Wilson, the headmaster. Andrew Whitton was chosen as praeses (or chairman) and James Wilson became clerk and Inspector of the Poor at £6 per year.

Funds were raised from the heritors and the inhabitants of the parish voluntarily. At first the Board had a deficit of £4 on January 1846, but by 1847 they had a credit balance of £13. It required £100 for six months' working. The Inspector asked for a raise to £10 per year, and got it. From 1848 funds were raised by assessment—assessors were appointed from the Board and James Wilson was appointed as Collector of Assessment at another £10 per year.

This assessment gave trouble. John Davidson of Kirkton farm, one of the assessors, could not agree with Andrew Whitton on the valuation of Couston at £350 and Davidston at £200. The other two assessors dodged the issue by claiming that they were appointed for the village only and not for the landward area.

There was also difficulty over assessing the Midland Junction Railway Co. who ran the line from Coupar Angus to Newtyle. Many other appeals were made against the assessment with varying results. The Board were fairly lenient with those too poor to pay—perhaps they had to be; after all if you cannot pay, you just cannot pay! The rent for a one-roomed house was £1 per year (later 'under £4') so the rate would be about 1½d per year. This rate varied according to the estimate for the year's working, and ranged over the years from 1d to 5d in £1. From 1869 onwards both proprietor and tenant paid the rate (e.g. 2d on proprietor and 2d on tenant).

Not all the paupers who were helped actually lived in Newtyle. Those who lived elsewhere had to establish either a five-year residence in Newtyle, or, of that could not be done, were born in Newtyle parish. This meant that other parishes were claiming on Newtyle, and Newtyle was claiming on other parishes.

One rather confusing incident happened in 1888. Robert Martin claimed on Newtyle—but there were two Robert Martins. Aboyne police notified Newtyle about the wrong one. This Scots Martin was a married man, decent and inoffensive. The other, an Irishman, was also married but was feared and known to the police. He was given nicknames such as 'Irish Bob'; 'Rob and his mither'; 'Thief Robert'; 'Needle Robert'; 'Daft Robert,' etc. To clear the matter up the Newtyle Inspector of the Poor (then John Jack) spent a week in Ireland and some days in Aboyne, at a cost of £40 for expenses, and it took over two years to clear the matter up.

On 7 April 1858 Andrew Murray of Ardler wrote the Board pleading that 'he would not keep his father any longer in his family' that 'he would feel obliged if the Board would cause him to be removed as soon as possible . . . I would give £10 with him.' There must have been some row going on in Murray's house at Ardler! The Board accepted his offer!

From 1845 to 1866 the number of poor supported by the Newtyle Board varied between 14 and 23; then rose until it was as high as 37 in 1870. By 1883 the number fell to 10 and finally in 1894 it was 7. For the 35 years from 1845 most of them lived in Newtyle parish, then there was a dramatic drop in 1887 to one Newtyle resident. This lasted until 1894 (none at all in 1893). There were always one or two in Dundee or Montrose Asylum.

The Board kept the odd room as a 'sick room' (locally known as the 'poorhouse') and paid a woman a few shillings a week to look after it. It was located at various times at Newbigging; in Church Street, Newtyle; and at Burnside.

In June 1848 a start was made to get two members elected from the public at a public meeting. The first two appointed were David Hill, farmer,

Bannatyne House; and George Moon, linen manufacturer, Newtyle. The meetings were now held in the school instead of the session house. Little or no interest was paid by the public in these elections, and during most of the years from 1864 to 1892, no electors turned up at the annual meetings. There is no evident reason for this apathy, but it could well be one of the factors which led to the replacement of Parochial Boards by Parish Councils.

Also in 1848 a start was made to expand the work of the parochial boards, when the Board of Supervisors in Edinburgh gave instructions for 'the more speedy removal of certain nuisances and the prevention of contagious and epidemic diseases.' The Newtyle Board set up a small committee to carry out the terms of the Act. They appointed a local practising surgeon, Dr Ure, as medical officer in charge, at £5 per year (later raised to £10) with reasonable allowances for medicines. The Board was entitled to a government grant if they spent a minimum sum of £9 4s 4d per year on medical relief of the poor. The medical officer's duties consisted of midwifery, and prompt and punctual attention to the medical needs of all poor persons. If the parish received a government grant the medical officer would be remunerated over and above his salary. Dr Ure professed himself dissatisfied with £10 per year and 'attending the birth of every child in Newtyle Parish.' So the Newtyle Board appointed Dr David M. Mills in August 1852 at £10 per year under the above conditions.

The Parochial Board also acted as sanitary inspectors and conditions in the village were reported annually. By 1853 most 'deplorable places' had been cleared and the rest 'would be soon.' Just as well because it was in this year that Dundee had its cholera epidemic. (It *was* known at the time that cholera was transmitted from one human to another only by direct contact with human excreta. The virus was not tracked down and isolated until about 1870).

The New Registration Act of 1854 made the appointment of a registrar for the parish necessary. The headmaster, James Wilson, was appointed with Dr Mills as his assistant.

By February 1863 houses lodging vagrants were to be licensed and inspected. There were three lodging houses in Newtyle at various times—Gallacher's in South Street; Anderson's in South Street; and Millar's in Castle Street. By 1871 none of these were in existence.

By September 1863 the Vaccination Act was introduced, and Dr Mills appointed as vaccinator for the parish.

In April 1864 James Wilson retired as inspector and John Jack was appointed at £10 per year. His many duties may have been too much for him, or for some other reason, a George S. Duncan became inspector of lodging houses and sanitary inspector.

In 1887 it was found that the water supply was bad and insufficient. The old pipe had been laid along the common street drain, so a new one was put in at a different alignment. The whole system was unsatisfactory, and the repairs by the heritors did little to better it. The Edinburgh Board of Supervisors wanted a more ambitious scheme put forward by their inspector, Mr Campbell. (It was not until January 1891 that the Dundee Water Commissioners extended their works, and a pipe-line passed through Newtyle parish, although none of this was fed to the village for some years).

Thirty-one proprietors had their own branch pipes from the main pipe and this had been carried out by different tradesmen. There must have been some indifferent work done, because of the considerable amount of water lost by leakage. There were two street wells and 20 householders had to carry water from them. They had '50 to 220 paces to go.' Despite this and other anomalies the parochial board recorded that the 'village and neighbourhood was still popular as a health resort.'

In April 1889 an Inspector of Dairies was appointed. Of course, John Jack was appointed, at £3 per year. There were five dairies in Newtyle, one of which was run by John Mustard, a railwayman, who had one 'coo.'

The amount of relief to the poor varied and seemed to depend on the cost of food. A fall in prices could mean a reduction in relief. It started in 1845 at 1/- plus 6d for each child per week. It was raised to 1/6 plus 9d per child in 1849; but it went down to 1/- plus 6d in 1864. The highest was 3/- from 1891 to 1895.

By 1888 poorhouse relief was offered instead of money—and to prevent a scandal the Inspector was instructed to offer poorhouse relief *in front of witnesses*. This Act was probably one of the most vicious ever passed by a government. The poor may have been poor but they could be proud, and the reputation of poorhouses did not encourage any to enter them unless they were at the lowest ebb of degradation. So—even in front of witnesses—the workhouse would be refused. We find, in March 1888, Alex Anderson was evicted and living out-of-doors, because he refused the poorhouse and therefore received no money. Someone took pity on him and he was residing at Hatton farm and looking after himself.

In June 1893 James Wilson retired as Registrar because of age and infirmity.

By May 1890 the new County Councils were set up, and Public Health was taken away from the parochial boards. In 1891 District Councils were set up, and Alex Bell of Davidstone farm became the representative from the parish. The Local Government (Scotland) Act of 1894 replaced the parochial board by the parish council. The Newtyle Parochial Board met for the last time on 16 March 1895.

Perhaps a few of the cases dealt with by the Newtyle Parochial Board may be of interest, in some if only for the language used.

'George Anderson, weaver, Newbigging had fallen into a state of violent excitement (mania). Paid watchers looked after him.'

'James Anderson, weaver, North Street, in 1851 asked for relief because of ill-health. He and his wife had been earning about 6/- per week between them. His claim was refused and he was advised to have his eldest daughter stay at home, and allow his wife, who was able-bodied, to go out and work.'

'In 1848 John Preston, weaver, Newtyle, was found to be lunatic and furious. He was committed to an asylum or some other place of safety.'

'In 1852 Henry Docherty, a travelling puddle-maker, and wife came to Newbigging. She was weak and found lying on straw in a barn. Newtyle gave relief, and were to prosecute the parish of Fossaway for that relief, but eventually compromised on £3 from Fossaway.'

'In May 1861 Peter Anderson, South Street, had been in a dumpish state of mind and submissive, but he became perfectly furious . . .'

'In November 1864 Agnes Adams or Garry, a travelling licensed hawker, in Gallacher's lodgings, gave birth to a male child. A few nights later she had left the parish.' (They were tough!!).

'In February 1865 Elizabeth Muir, a travelling woman, died in Gallacher's lodgings. She had been visited by the medical officer, who thought she was suffering from cold and weakness.'

The Newtyle Parish Council 1895-1930 [74]

There is a gap in the records from 1895 to 1926. One detail has come to light so far. They kept a small house in Church Street as a sick room, or 'poorhouse' as it was known locally.

By December 1926 the Council met in the schoolroom. Alex Millar, the baker, was chairman, and Mr Whitton was the representative to the District Committee of the County Council. But a year later Mr Millar retired from the chair because of ill-health and W. R. Macdonald of Kirkton House took his place.

The Inspector, Clerk and Registrar, William Irvine, the headmaster, retired in July 1927, and the new headmaster, Henry Joiner, took his place.

There were between 3 and 5 poor being supported in Newtyle. There must have been others, probably vagrants, because just over £200 was raised annually by rating, plus a grant of £15 from the Scottish Office.

The casual sick room in Church Street was run by a Mrs Fraser—a note records that she received £4 8s 3d for food for vagrants in March 1927. By March 1928 she had moved to Dundee, and a Mrs Langlands took her place, only to be replaced in June 1929 by Mrs Margaret Langlands.

There were so few items during this period that one is left with the feeling that the secretary of the Council did not record the detail which his predecessor of the Parochial Board had done.

In December 1926 there was an arrangement between the Parish Council and the tenant of Kirkton House about dumping rubbish (i.e. grass mowings) from the kirkyard into Kirkton's grounds. This cropped up quite a few times right up to the 1960s. In March 1927 a gale blew down the stones in the kirkyard.

In October 1927 the Council advertised for a caretaker of drainage and waterworks, lamplighter, gravedigger, etc., at £78 per year. They got four applicants. This was the start of employing a 'village officer.' In the same year Henry Joiner became clerk to the Graveyard Committee at £5 per year.

By June 1928 Newtyle became a Special Scavenging District, and there was also word of Local Government changes. The new County Council took over in May 1930, but the Inspector was to remain in office for six months.

At the end of the Parish Council the members were—W. R. Macdonald, chairman; W. K. Sim; Alex Millar (who had been a member since the beginning); and Cecil B. Shields—four in all plus the Inspector.

Chapter 4

EDUCATION

The earliest record of teaching is of a John Christie who taught Latin in 1690 in Newtylle [98]. In 1717 it is recorded that there was no schoolmaster in the parish. George Browster was parish schoolmaster from 1786 to 1838—a total of 52 years teaching in Newtyle plus another 15 or so years teaching before he came to Newtyle. He died on 17 February 1838 *still teaching* at the age of 82, and is buried in Newtyle kirkyard.

By the 1840s there seems to have been two schools in Newtyle. A Mr Robertson was a teacher about 1840 in what was probably the boys' school in North Street (the parish school). At Kirkton Miss Eliza K. Stevenson started in the 'female school' in 1846. This could well have been on the site of what is known as West Cottage in Coupar Angus Road, or somewhere near there. A 'female school' was a girls' school, whereas a 'dame school' was a school run by a 'dame' or woman teacher, with a mixed class of boys and girls, usually about the infant stage. These teachers had no qualifications, and in some cases very little education. They earned a meagre living by charging a copper or two per pupil. In 1843 James Wilson became the teacher in the parish school.

It is doubtful if these early schools could give much education, not even the three Rs. Very little writing was taught. Most of the teaching was by rote, with the class taking part by repetition individually or in unison. There would be no blackboards and little or no furniture—seats and/or desks. Only a few could be taught writing, and that would be done with a slate and a slate pencil or skaillie. It was with extreme difficulty that the parish school about 1850 could get forms (never mind desks) for the scholars to sit on, and it was not uncommon to find pupils lying on the floor writing. Paper was scarce and poor in quality. Pupils seldom, if ever, used it. Books were few and far between. Those that were available were well-thumbed, well-used, tattered and torn. They were shared and any new books were given to the best pupils.

The Belmont Sale Catalogue [116] of 1872 had an infant school and schoolhouse in hand next to the smiddy at the old Kirkton farm, but there is no further indication of what happened to it. There is some hearsay evidence that the lodge at Bannatyne House was used as a school and schoolhouse, but there is no concrete evidence.

So, by 1873 we have the female school at Kirkton run by Miss Eliza K. Stevenson, and the parish school in North Street with James Wilson as teacher. (The title headmaster came later).

The Newtyle School Board [78]

The Education Grant Act of 1833 made a grant for elementary education for the first time. The 1870 Elementary Education Act established

School Boards with powers to levy an education rate and compelled the attendance of all children between 5 and 13 years of age. Parents paid fees but these could be remitted by the Board in cases of need. The Cowper-Temple clause provided Bible teaching at the option of the parents.

On 3 May 1873 the School Board of the Parish of Newtyle held its first meeting in the schoolroom. The members who were elected at a public meeting in April were:

Rev. George Brown, parish minister.

Rev. John Fleming, free church minister.

Rev. John Muir, united presbyterian minister.

George Smith Duncan, elder.

James Mill Robertson, elder.

Note the predominance of the church and the effect this would have on the Cowper-Temple clause of the Act.

There were two nominations for the post of secretary and treasurer—John Jack and George S. Duncan. The latter was appointed, and had to find security for £200.

Salaries were:

Miss Stevenson	—	£70 per year.
Mr Wilson	—	£55 plus part of government grant.
Mr Duncan	—	£10 per year.

£150 was to be raised by assessment—this left £15 plus part of the grant to pay for cleaner, rent of the female school and the upkeep of the two schools.

Her Majesty's Inspector of Schools paid a prompt visit. He reported that the schools were well run, but they were insufficient for the needs of the parish, and the school apparatus was inferior.

The Board set out to enlarge the parish school and incorporate the female school in it. The first plan, made by Mr Davidson, architect, Belmont Castle, was to cost £750. This was sent back for reconsideration as it was thought by the Board to cost too much. Further plans were approved, but it took over a year to get permission from the Scotch Education Department, London, to go ahead. The Board also had to get permission to borrow £1,200 repaid over 35 years. The Department gave a grant of £202 0s 10d. The Board borrowed £1,000 from the Public Works Loan Board at $3\frac{1}{2}\%$ repaid over 35 years at £50 per year, and the balance in the 35th year. In effect—this was an extension on both sides of the old school rather than a new school. To carry out the work Lord Wharncliffe gifted extra ground.

The contractors were:

J. & D. Gray, masons, Newtyle.

John Jack, joiner, Newtyle.

John Butchart, slater, Kirkinch.

A. Laing & Sons, plumbers, Coupar Angus.

Peter Donaldson, plasterer, Coupar Angus.

James Marshall, painter, Coupar Angus.

David Hardie, blacksmith, Newtyle.

The total cost was £1,299 1s 11½d, plus £96 3s 8d for gas, water, boundary walls and fences. They also built a 2-foot dyke in front of the school, and a railing to divide the two playgrounds. There was also a date stone over the centre window—'Newtyle Public School 1875.' The school was opened on 18 October 1875.

The two schools were now amalgamated in the one building but operated separately for some years to come. The female school and school-house were given up. Miss Stevenson was to teach the infants while the male teacher did the rest.

The school was used for meetings and functions in the village, such as the 8th Forfarshire Rifle Volunteers; the Library Committee; Newtyle Literary Society; and Kinpurney Lodge of Good Templars. In November the Good Templars ran an evening of readings from Burns illustrated by 'dissolving views.'

James Wilson, the parish teacher, was asked to retire because of age. He did so, accepting £45 per year with the house in North Street rent-free. There were eleven applicants for the post. Peter Fergusson from Callander was successful. He started in March 1874 at £140 per year, including 'fees and grants.' On his request maps were purchased and furniture repaired. Any school or copy books were to be obtained from Mr Wilson.

School fees were discussed and the following scale made out:

1st class—reading; writing; arithmetic; geography; grammar; history	4/– per quarter
2nd class—same without history	3/6 ,, ,,
3rd class—as 2nd class	3/– ,, ,,
4th class—as 2nd class	2/6 ,, ,,
5th class—as 2nd class	2/6 ,, ,,
6th class—infants	1/6 ,, ,,

Latin or French additional at 1/– per quarter extra;
or Both with mathematics at 2/– per quarter extra.

Pupil teachers were appointed in 1874—Alex Watt, Newton of Auchter-house, and William John Duncan, Newtyle. By this time the roll of the school was about 150. So Mr Fergusson had over 100 pupils in his class. The two pupil teachers would be a help. They received about £4 per year plus their education.

The Board also appointed Thomas Saunders as an Officer of the Board (attendance officer) at £2 5s 0d per year; Annie Fitchie as school cleaner; and Peter Mitchell as janitor at £2 10s 0d per year. Teachers' hours of work were reduced from 6 to 5 hours, and Miss Stevenson was asked to give one hour's instruction in sewing daily. This was the start of getting away from the daily grind of only the three Rs.

In November a Miss Catherine Stevenson was appointed sewing mistress at £14 per year. The Board also offered Sergeant O'Shaughnessy, drill instructor, Newtyle, the sum of £3 3s 0d per year to give the boys half an hour drill two days a week before and after school hours. But he declined.

On the night of 21/22 November 1875 a fire started in one of the class-rooms. Its origin does not seem to be known, but the damage was not sufficient to interrupt school work.

Elections were held in the school on 20 May 1876 for a new Board. Mr G. S. Duncan (now living in Blairgowrie) was Returning Officer. The new Board which met on Saturday 30 May at 3 p.m. were:

1. Rev. John Fleming, Free Church (Chairman).
2. Edward Howatt, merchant, Bannatyne House.
3. Rev. George Bell Lunan, Parish Church.
4. James Mill Robertson, merchant, North Street.
5. Andrew Whitton, Couston House.

In 1877 sheds were put up in the playground at a cost of £19 10s 0d (assume two sheds) and blackboards were bought for the classrooms. A communicating door was also made between the two schools. This opened the way, when the opportunity arose, to make it one school and appoint a headmaster.

By March 1878 music was taught by Mr Justice, music teacher, Dundee, at 5/- per hour. Later in 1879 a Mr Honeyman taught the violin on Saturday evenings. He also arranged concerts and held rehearsals in the school. One of these concerts was by the pupils of Mr Neil of Forfar (the well-known 'Dancie Neil'). The same Thomas Honeyman started the Newtyle Musical Society on 2 October 1880. They gave annual concerts in the school. About 1882-3 this Society seems to have gone defunct.

On 29 March 1878 John Henry complained about Miss Stevenson's punishment of his son. The Board warned the teachers about punishment on the head. They supplied each teacher with a belt or tawse, and insisted that punishment be on the hand only. John Henry also complained in June of the same year that some pupils were told by the teachers to stay at home during the visit of Her Majesty's Inspector. Mr Fergusson was able to explain about the attendance of the two boys—Christy and Horn. He produced copies of H.M.I's report showing that both boys were at the examination.

There seems to have been some trouble about the pigsty and privy (outside lavatory) in the schoolhouse garden (occupied by Mr Wilson). The complaint came from James M. Robertson next door. The Sanitary Inspector (John Jack) gave them a clean bill of health and Mr Wilson won the day.

Teachers in 1879 were asked to give quarterly reports about the pupils—on cards.

The clerk and treasurer—G. S. Duncan—resigned in March 1882. There were three applicants for the job—Alex Phin, accountant; John Jack, Inspector of the Poor; and James M. Robertson. Mr Phin was appointed at £10 per year. One does wonder if the Board had any animosity against John Jack because he wanted to be Jack-of-all-trades, and J. M. Robertson because of the complaint about the schoolhouse. This is only conjecture.

On 1 October 1882 Mr Fergusson resigned because of ill-health. There were five applicants from Dundee, Fife and Glasgow, but J. D. Morgan from Aberdeen was appointed at £75 plus two-thirds of the government grant. He got a school bell, an alarm spring-top bell, a map of the county of Forfar, a modulator for music, and a foot-scraper at each entrance to the school.

41

In 1883 an effort was made to introduce agricultural education. A letter from Lord Dalhousie offered to send an officer from the Science and Art Department of South Kensington Museum, London, to explain the government's intention. It was decided that Mr Morgan go to Kensington on a short course.

In 1884 Mr Phin of the Commercial Bank was posted elsewhere and resigned as secretary/treasurer. Mr Dickson, clerk to the bank was appointed in his place. John Jack tried again but failed. Mr Dickson left the district in 1885 and he was succeeded by Mr J. A. Webster, bank agent. John Jack tried again, but this time he was given the job as School Board Officer.

The new Board elected in May 1885 consisted of:

> Alex Bell, farmer, Davidston.
> William Findlay, grocer, Newtyle.
> John Henry, manure merchant, Newtyle.
> Rev. G. B. Lunan, parish minister.
> Andrew Whitton, Couston (Chairman).

In December 1886 Miss Robertson, an assistant teacher, resigned. There were 31 applicants. The post was offered to a Miss Hardie, but she had accepted a job elsewhere. A Miss Slidders was appointed at £40 per year. She gave so much trouble with her continued and repeated absence that she was dismissed. When the job was re-advertised there were 24 applicants. Miss Cree was given the job at £35 per year to start.

The Board decided that the school should open one hour earlier in the morning—the new time to be 9.30 a.m.

To celebrate the Queen's Jubilee in 1887, Mr Whitton presented a Silver Jubilee Medal to the best scholar; Mr Findlay and Mr Bell between them presented another—so one for a boy and one for a girl. In 1888 a school soup kitchen was started at a cost of £35. The inspection of religious education was also started.

In January 1889 Mr George Gray complained of the filthy nature of the school. Dr Smith was called in, and he reported on the families he had visited. He found in three of them 'body and head lice in large numbers due to the want of cleanliness.' He suggested the use of carbolic soap and 'precipitate ointment'—also the clothes to be disinfected. The school itself was inspected by John Jack, Sanitary Inspector, and Dr Smith. It was closed on 28 January for scrubbing and disinfecting. The houses of Chapman and Bunch at Newbigging were so filthy that they were brought to the attention of the Parochial Board, who were asked to contact the Board of Supervisors in Edinburgh. Chapman left the district in May 1889, but Mrs Bunch was still being warned in June that 'if her children were not sent to school in a respectably clean state by Wednesday 12 June, she would be brought before the Sheriff.'

The Education Act of 1891 brought free education to the elementary school. The Newtyle Board operated this when the school started after the holidays in October. On instruction from the County Council of Forfarshire, the Board started to think about classes in agriculture, cookery and technical subjects. They were also asked to submit suggestions as to centres of higher education.

Changes were happening in the village itself between 1891 and 1893—the streets were to be lit (the school railing was to be used for a lamp-post); a new water supply was put in; there was a meeting of the feuars about the insanitary state of the village; and efforts were made to clean up the school and ventilate it better.

On the death of Mr Wilson, the Board had some difficulty over the schoolhouse in North Street. Mr Malloch's house next door had a bedroom over the wash-house of the schoolhouse, and a small conservatory overlooking and jutting into the schoolhouse garden. Mr Malloch had no access to his garden except through his house, and he offered to buy the wash-house to give him access. The Board refused and even put in a lath and plaster ceiling in the wash-house. The whole schoolhouse in 1894 was in poor condition. New floors, new drains, inside w.c. and bathroom, and a porch, were all installed at a cost of £175.

New title deeds for the schoolhouse were made up after a lot of discussion over the dividing wall and Mr Malloch's conservatory. The Board objected to insinuation of interference with Mr Malloch's 'lights.' In 1897 the work was at last carried out. Mr Morgan married that year and occupied the house rent-free for the duration of his term of office as headmaster. The school was given a hoiday for a week starting 15 November on the occasion of the marriage.

1895 saw the resignation of Miss Louise Jack having been teaching at Newtyle for a year and a half. Miss Janet Dingwall was appointed. She was the daughter of the gardener who lived at 'Achterneed' in North Street. Mr Webster, the clerk, left the district in May and, at last, John Jack was appointed clerk at £10 per year; but he had to resign as Compulsory Officer. The new officer was Robert Fenwick, the letter deliverer, at £5 per year.

In December 1895 the Board met in Mr Cumming's office at 1 Bank Street, Dundee. He advised them to accept the offer by the Earl of Wharncliffe of a feu of 6d per year in perpetuity for the school house. The Rev. G. B. Lunan objected because by the Act of 1803 the ground was freehold. But the Board accepted the offer.

Slowly but surely the powers-that-be were becoming conscious of sanitation and environment. In 1898 the school was closed for three weeks from 3 January because of a measles epidemic. The building was disinfected. Mumps were epidemic in 1902, measles in 1904, and scarlet fever in 1906. The lavatories were in a mess. It cost £20 to clear the drains. The narrow strip of woodland round three sides of the school became a danger to health, as it was treated by the villagers as a free coup or dump. This had been going on for years, and in 1902, after consultations with Dr Barty, factor to the Earl of Wharncliffe, the School Board took over responsibility for the strip. They cleaned it out and levelled it. This also allowed for an extension to the playground.

Evening classes were being run in the school from 1898 mainly in dressmaking. A grant of £8 was received for that purpose, and the charge was 6d per night for the janitor. By 1902 the County Council made Newtyle a centre for cooking and laundry classes, as well as lectures in agriculture.

Meigle, Eassie and Newtyle schools held a conference in April 1899 to decide on uniformity of holidays and school books. Other schools had discontinued drill by army instructors and allowed the teachers to do it.

Physical and military drill in school was a recommendation from the Secretary of State for Scotland. Newtyle had carried on for a number of years using Sergeant Instructor Winn of Glamis at £4 per session. In August 1901 Sgt. Winn resigned, and then the Board decided that the teachers do it. Incidently, John Reid, 'professor of dancing' applied for the job.

In August 1901 Margaret Leuchars, a blind pupil staying with her parents at Couston, was sent to the Blind Institution, Dundee, at a cost of £5 per year, with her parents' consent. But by December her parents withdrew her from the Institution, and she returned to Newtyle school to pick up 'such tuition as she can.' No reason was given.

In May 1899 a new Code was issued recommending that drawing and nature study be included in the day school curriculum, and the Board decided to get the apparatus. Black linoleum was fixed to the walls of the classrooms for free-hand drawing. Miss Dingwall was sent to drawing classes in Forfar and Dundee. Mr Morgan also asked for a piano, but there is no indication whether he got it or not.

In 1901 there was a change in teachers' salaries. The headmaster received £155 per year irrespective of the government grant. Teachers no longer got a retiral allowance from the Board, but contributed to the Teachers' Superannuation Fund. Mr Morgan asked the Board to relieve Miss Stevenson of her contribution to the fund, as she was so near retiral. Her pay was then increased by £2 (the contribution) to £57 per year. Also Miss Dingwall's salary was raised from £40 to £50 per year.

Queen Victoria died in 1901 and the Board sent a letter of sympathy to King Edward VII. For the coronation celebrations the school had a holiday on 26 and 27 June: the chairman, Andrew Whitton of Couston, presented each scholar with a Coronation medal: and the Board were to discuss some celebration with the Parish Council.

After the 1903 elections the composition of the Board was:

> Andrew Whitton, Couston.
> William Findlay, grocer, Millhouse.
> Robert Sim, merchant, Mundamalla.
> James Soutar, medical practitioner.
> Rev. G. B. Lunan, parish minister.
> John Jack, clerk.

Miss Eliza K. Stevenson, infant mistress, was to have retired on 12 March 1906, but she was allowed to continue until 30 June. She died on 9 June having served 33 years with the Board, and at least 60 years as a teacher in Newtyle. She must have been ill for the last few months because Miss Jane L. McFarlane was appointed interim teacher, then Miss Marjorie Beaton from Meigle was appointed assistant. Miss Dingwall was transferred to be in charge of the infant department.

Andrew Whitton retired from the Board in April 1906 because of ill-health, after 30 years as chairman.

In 1906 there was trouble with the school buildings and infectious diseases. Donald and Donaldson ventilators were installed in the walls of the classrooms, with Buchan Patent Ceiling Valves as outlets. The lavatories were filthy and the drains choked. Coal and firewood were stored under the galleries of the classrooms. The school was closed on 18 June because of scarlet fever (even Miss Dingwall took the disease).

New furniture was installed—blackboards for the junior division; a desk and press or cupboard for the headmaster's room; 25 dual desks in oak for the infant room; the main room was divided by a moveable partition; the infant rooms were re-floored; plumber work was carried out; maps and a clock were bought.

In December 1907 John Jack died, and in January 1908 James Keay, jnr. was appointed clerk to the Board. In 1909 the Board considered a small garden for the school, but it was two years before it was started. Assistance and demonstrations were given by the East of Scotland College of Agriculture, and classes were started on Mondays, Wednesdays and Fridays from 3 to 4 p.m.

A new heating system was installed in the school in November 1909—hot water pipes and radiators in three large and two small classrooms at a cost of £110. In October 1911 there was a fire in the boiler house. The whole of the wooden structure round the boiler was replaced with steel and cement. New floors and new desks were put into the larger classrooms.

Miss Beaton went off ill in November 1909 with scarlet fever. In April 1911 Miss Dingwall became ill and was given one month's leave of absence. But it was over a year before she returned, her place being taken by a student from University College, Dundee. But she took ill again in October 1914, and did not return until April 1916.

In 1909 some of the older pupils went with County Council bursaries to Harris Academy, Dundee. Potato-planting time in April each year saw a drop in attendance. In summer the pupils were at berry-picking, and 4/5 weeks seemed to be the usual holidays in July/August with another 4 weeks in September/October for harvest and potato-picking.

The clerk resigned in April 1911 and Charles Ballantine was appointed at £10 per year. That year saw the Coronation of King George V. Celebrations were held and on 26 June, James Coates of Paisley (of thread fame) presented each scholar in Scotland with a schoolbag. On 30 June the school was closed to allow the headmaster to attend a course in school gardening. On 22 December 1911, the chemical works or 'bone mill' closed down with a resultant drop in the school roll.

In 1912 the school was closed because of an epidemic of measles. The pupils got another day's holiday when the headmaster was cited to attend the Sheriff Court in Alloa. Scarlet fever closed the school in February 1914.

On 15 September 1914 the clerk resigned and Alex E. Gray was appointed at £10 per year. A piano was at last purchased in February 1914.

The military authorities commandeered the school buildings in October 1915 to billet one battery of the 2nd/1st Royal Field Artillery, Highland Brigade. The school used the old Free Church in Belmont Street (later the British Legion Hall) at a rent of £2 per month. The existing pews were removed and additional lavatories and heating installed. The lighting was so bad that classes were dismissed early, and the street was used as a playground. Some of the soldiers' children from Aberdeen attended the school.

The army gave the school back in May 1916, making good any damage, and sharing the cost of re-decoration with the Board. It was found too difficult to replace the pews in the old church, and, in agreement with the Deacons Court, the wood of the pews was used to make forms. £70 was received from the army for the rent of the school during their occupation.

Miss Beaton resigned in November 1916 to go to China to be married, and her place was taken by Miss Kate A. Duncan from Coupar Angus. The Board appointed the local policeman, Andrew Spence, as Attendance Officer. It took more than six months for the Chief Constable to find out and put his foot down.

War bonuses were given in 1917—£7 10s 0d to each member of the staff and £1 to the caretaker—for 1 year only. But the end of the war saw an improvement in the scale of salaries, passed by the Scottish Education Department, helped by the Educational Institute of Scotland—Mr Morgan £195; Miss Jeffrey £95; and Miss Dingwall £85. Salaries were now paid monthly by cheque instead of quarterly.

December 1918 saw an epidemic of influenza and Newtyle school was closed for a fortnight. In May 1919 Dr Mills left £300 to the Parish Council and the School Board, the income from which was to be used in the park.

The final meeting of the Newtyle School Board took place on 9 May 1919. The Fisher Education Act of 1918—

abolished all fees;

made education compulsory up to 14 years, and compulsory Day Continuation Schools up to age 16 and after 7 years to 18 (exemptions were given after age 14);

no child under 13 to be employed;

widened the idea of education—e.g. clinics, open-air schools, medical inspections.

School Management Committee

School Management Committees were formed. The parishes of Eassie, Newtyle, Ruthven and Kettins were incorporated as District No. 11 [79]. This arrangement lasted until 1936 when Ruthven was disjoined from Newtyle, etc., and added to Lintrathen District.

The first meeting of the S.M.C. was held in Newtyle school on 29 September 1919 with Thomas Wedderspoon of Castleton as chairman (he represented the Education Authority); James C. Guild of Kirkton represented the parents; and Thomas Pitkeathly, Belmont Street, from the local bodies. The staff of the school were—James D. Morgan, headmaster; Elizabeth Gilchrist and Janet M. Dingwall. The clerk to the Committee was T. C. Lowson, solicitor, Forfar, at £40 per year.

Mr Morgan retired and the new headmaster, William Irvine, started in August 1920. In December 1921 a soup kitchen was started at a cost of £45 and about 50 children took advantage of it. This increased to 65 by 1926.

There were some complaints about books in 1922. Many parents worked on farms. Feeing and tied houses meant that there was a continual movement from farm to farm. Because of this parents found that they were

46

buying books for one school, then moving house to another area, where they had to buy other books for another school. So they were refusing to buy school books. The S.M.C. wrote the Executive Officer suggesting a uniform system of books for rural schools.

On 20 January 1922 the school was closed because of a bad storm—only three pupils turned up. Both the headmaster and Miss Gilchrist were ill. This year also saw a holiday for the Royal wedding; a talk on 'Care of baby' by Mrs Barnett, Aberdeen; and the Qualifying Examination for the top primary class on 26 May. (This examination, mainly in English and Arithmetic, decided whether a pupil went to a Grammar School or not).

In 1923 the S.M.C. in their wisdom thought that fire extinguishers were not necessary in school. But they were over-ruled by the Education Authority, and agreed to put in one per school. In 1924 there were set out four leaving dates—1 February; 1 May; 1 August and 1 November. Up to now pupils could leave on their 14th birthday.

The General Strike of May 1926 seemed to have little impact on Newtyle. There were no trains and one teacher was absent.

Mr Irvine retired and Henry Joiner from Glamis became headmaster in August 1927. That same year two of the classrooms were made into three rooms by a moveable partition. Workshop tools and science equipment arrived. This was augmented by the loan of a rain gauge and maximum/minimum thermometer from Mervyn E. H. Burnett of the bulb farm. Alex Millar also gave the hand-bell that belonged to Mr Robertson, schoolmaster in Newtyle at the time of the Disruption (c1840).

The school was closed in June 1928 because of an outbreak of diphtheria, when the headmaster's own son died of it. By October a new drainage system was put in. Road signs were placed at each end of the school grounds; and a scheme of grants was outlined by the Education Authority to buy equipment for organised games. For the first time a school fund was started by a concert in the Wharncliffe Hall. The Education Authority bought the old U.F. manse in Church Street (next the hall) as a headmaster's house.

Schools and education had improved very slowly since the beginning of the century. It was still slow—in 1931 suggestions were put forward for additional accommodation. One room was used as an ordinary classroom as well as for cookery, technical work, science and art. It was all deferred. Eventually in 1935 a new building containing two classrooms, toilets and cloakrooms, was erected in line with the old building. This became the infant school.

Two incidents of interest are recorded in the school log book of 1937:

January 11—Miss Roy was late (almost 10 minutes) in arriving at school, and the headmaster advised her to be on time in the morning.

January 18—The headmaster received a telegram from Glenshee to say that Miss Roy was unavoidably detained there, rescuing mountain climbers lost in the snow.

February 1939 saw preparations in case of war—the school was closed for three days to allow the staff to conduct a house survey for evacuation purposes. Miss Mitchell was given three days' leave in July to attend a course in Glasgow on mass cookery. Milk supply was re-started to the scholars—and, at last, in 1940 the old school was wired for electricity.

In August 1939 five mothers, five pre-school children, 26 pupils and 6 teachers (from the Morgan Academy, Dundee) were evacuated to Newtyle from Dundee. Miss Isobel Gray, teacher in the Morgan Academy, and resident in Newtyle, was in charge of infants and juniors (now numbering 45). Miss Kirk of Harris Academy, Dundee, was to teach English and French to secondary evacuees. Mr Charles Johnston from Logie School was to teach mathematics and science.

In November 1939 James D. Morgan died. He was headmaster from 1885 to 1920 (35 years).

After the New Year holidays several evacuees did not return. They gradually dwindled down until by 1942 only three were left.

The 4th July 1940 saw the scare of enemy landings by parachute, and the local policeman advised dismissing the school. 'The pupils showed great spirit and acted promptly without any alarm.' (School log book).

In 1941 the new two-classroom building was being used by the Polish army as hospital and dental surgery. This meant five classes in four rooms. The infants were dismissed at 1 p.m. each day.

The Education Act of 1944 raised the school leaving age to fifteen.

Henry Joiner retired as headmaster on 31 March 1945, and William W. Colvin from Craichie school took his place. Newtyle was now to become a rural secondary school, and in 1947 pupils were transferred from Kinnettles, Glamis, Eassie and Kettins to the secondary department at Newtyle—if they failed the 11+ examination. This meant the introduction of specialist teachers, some of whom were itinerant (coming to Newtyle for one or a few days per week). Academic pupils were still sent to either Dundee or Forfar. The Wharncliffe Hall was used for school meals, and at last the room used for technical, domestic, art and science, was converted into a technical room. A new two-room temporary building was erected for science and domestic science.

Note on bibliography—Neither of the following mention Newtyle school:
History of the burgh and parish schools of Scotland, by James Grant, 1876.
Education in Angus, by J. C. Jessop, 1931.

Libraries—the Newtyle Public Library

When the new village was planned in 1832 a pamphlet or brochure was issued eulogising the site as having the ability to 'grow and flourish.' 'Further to induce purchasers, certain privileges were promised, and among others, that of a Reading Room and Library. None of these privileges promised were ever more heard of' (John Jack). Many of those who came to Newtyle were weavers from the village of Lochee and the environments of Dundee. These 'incomers' were an intelligent class of men, and they were well-versed in the events of the time—the Reform Bill and the struggle for the abolition of the Corn Laws. This was despite their educational disadvantages and the slowness of news, often carried by packmen or passing strangers. They were avaricious readers when they got the chance and were politically Chartists.

Literature of any description was scarce and dear, beyond the range of the poor weaver whose income might range from 7s 6d to 12s per week, when they had a 'web in the loom.' Chambers' Journal, Chambers' Penny Tracts, a Dundee newspaper costing 4d a copy (this included 1d for the Inland Revenue)—these were 'clubbed for' and each was passed on from hand to hand, every word being read and digested.

To meet the need for other books, a James Stewart (better known as Moley Stewart—he was a mole-catcher) opened a small library in one of the rooms of his house, and loaned out books. The labels on his books read:

JAMES STEWART'S

CIRCULATING LIBRARY

NEW VILLAGE . . . Newtyle

Terms—One penny each volume per week;

New Books twopence per week;

or 1s 3d per quarter in total.

Price if lost or destroyed £0 8s 6d.

All library payments to be made in advance.

After a few years Moley Stewart left the village and took his library with him.

A short time after Stewart's removal, Mr Jack (John's father) opened a circulating library in his house in Church Street. He had an arrangement with second-hand booksellers in Dundee and Coupar Angus, whereby the books were exchanged now and again. They seldom, if ever, were new.

This library was open in the evenings and Mr Jack entrusted the position of librarian to his son, John, then a schoolboy. John Jack admits to 'poring over some of these books, at the sacrifice of my school tasks; while often for doing so I paid the penalty by suffering the infliction of something stronger and fully more convincing than moral suasion.'

The books at that time were by such authors as Walter Scott; Captain Marryat; W. Harrison Ainsworth; J. Fennimore Cooper; Charles Dickens; with, in addition, the histories of Scotland and its heroes; 'Tales of the borders'; Chambers' Journal; Hogg's Instructor. The library ended shortly after the death of Mr Jack, senior, in 1852.

One evening in 1855 in the parlour of Alexander Millar's house four people met—Rev. Quentin Johnstone (probationer assistant to Rev. John Moon), James W. Robertson, Andrew Whitton, and John Jack. Out of this meeting sprang the idea of starting a library on a different basis from private enterprise. After a number of informal meetings when others joined the group—Rev. John Muir of the Secession Church, and Rev. James Clark, probationer of the Free Church—a public meeting was held in the Secession church (later the Wharncliffe Hall). After much discussion a committee was formed. Subscription lists were opened, a constitution drawn up, and the library opened on 31 March 1856 with about 60 books.

At the first annual meeting in 1857 the income from subscriptions, charges to readers, etc., totalled £53 most of which had been spent on books. There was a printed constitution with a catalogue of some 200 books.

Mr Johnstone left the village, and, at last, Rev. John Moon, parish minister, began to take some interest. 'He was not a progressive man among us' (John Jack). The committee widened their interests by running concerts during the winter session, two of them adding £8 10s 0d to the funds.

A series of lectures were run and we find:

Course of lectures—10d.   Single lecture—2d.

1858-9 George Gilfillan, Dundee. 'The general characteristic of the Age.'
Rev. R. Cowan. 'Columbus, his life, time and discovery.'
Rev. A. Ross, Rattray. 'Scotland under the Stuarts.'
Rev. John Muir. 'The pursuit of knowledge with difficulties.'
Rev. R. Russell, Rattray. 'Home, what makes and mars.'
Mr J. Brodie, student, Dunkeld. (who has been blind from infancy). 'Self-knowledge.'

These lectures started at 8 p.m.

1860   Debate—Which benefits man—inventor or the improver?
1894   Mr Ostler of Kintyre, agricultural correspondent to the *Courier*, Dundee. 'My recent tour of America.'
1896   'Peoples' Friend' series of lantern slides.
1898   D. B. Salmond, Glasgow. 'A trip to Transvaal.'

The committee also held penny readings, spelling bees and drama.

Now and again donations were received, for example:

The Misses Lyall (sisters of Sir Charles Lyall, the geologist) when they left Drumkilbo, presented about 100 volumes from their private library.

The firm of Messrs. Moon and Langlands, drapers, Albion House, Dundee, sent a large number of books which they had for the use of their employees, who boarded in the house.

1898   Donation of 21s from Lord Strathcona, High Commissioner for Canada, through Mr C. S. Arnton.
1898   Offer of £5 annually from Mr Andrew Carnegie on condition that the library became free. This was refused.
1903   20 April.   9/- donated from the defunct Newtyle Musical Association.
1910   Sir Charles W. Cayzer, Kinpurnie Castle, donated 100 books.
1920   Legacy of £25 from Mrs Mills and £100 from Dr D. M. Mills.
(The interest on this is still being used).

The library was first located in the parish school with the teacher, Mr Wilson, as librarian. This lasted only a short time then the books were stocked in the corner of the Free Church in Belmont Street, with Alexander Buttar, a Free Church teacher, as secretary and librarian. He removed to Dundee and John Jack became librarian in 1858.

Its new home now became a small loft in Belmont Street where it stayed until it was removed to the Wharncliffe Hall in 1885. Access to the old loft was by an outside stair, but this was partly demolished in the 1960s leaving a single-storey shed.

About 1926 the library started to receive a supply of books from the County Library. These would arrive periodically in boxes, which could, if wished, once the lid was removed, be set up as lockable bookcases. This was often done in schools and other places in the rural parts of Angus. The library room in the Wharncliffe Hall had the walls lined with lockable bookcases, where both the County Library books and those belonging to the local library, were stored. The local committee sent an annual donation of £3 to the County Library.

In 1906 the library celebrated its jubilee by having a concert which raised £7 4s 0d. It also celebrated the jubilee of John Jack's services; and John himself celebrated by writing and printing the history of the Newtyle library. Most of the material for this history comes from that publication, and from Henry Joiner's article in the *Evening Telegraph* in 1956.

During this first 50 years the library had its struggles and bad times. We find that Mr Whitton of Couston, trustee for the Wharncliffe Hall, fixed the rent at £3 per week plus coal, light and cleaning, for one hour. The library committee at the time suggested £1 rent and 10/- for coal, etc. No agreement was reached and the library stayed in the old loft instead of moving to the hall earlier.

Agreement must have been reached in 1885 as the library was moved into a room in the hall. The committee were very proud of the wire gauze screen covering part of the window. On it was painted 'Newtyle Public Library.'

In 1886 the treasurer, J. M. Robertson, removed to Dundee without handing over the funds amounting to £2 11s 7½d. This was 'written off' in 1890 after many attempts to get it back.

In 1895 the committee considered asking the Parish Council to take over the library under the Public Libraries Act of 1887 and the Local Government Act of 1894. This never seems to have happened. Perhaps by 1895 the library was financially better off and preferred to remain independent.

By 1898 they were in difficulties, and they approached Mr Whitton to lower the rent. The trouble was not only money but lack of public interest. We find the following typical entry in the minutes—'A.G.M. 1899. Office-bearers re-elected. They were all that was present.'

John Jack died in 1907 and his place as librarian was taken by James D. Morgan, headmaster. By 1910 the stock had amounted to 2,435 books and shelf-space became a problem. Some 500 books were weeded out and a new catalogue printed at a cost of £10.

The war of 1914-18 put a check on the activities because the hall had been commandeered by the military authorities.

In 1920 William Irvine became headmaster and took James Morgan's place on the library committee. Alex Millar, the baker, was librarian from 1918 to his death in 1929. Miss Rose Jeffrey was his assistant from 1922 to 1924. Two ministers took a very active interest in the library, especially in cataloguing the books. They were the Rev. George Lunan and the Rev. John Mechie.

James Fenwick, the blacksmith, was its librarian from 1929 to 1970. Henry Joiner, headmaster, was a member of the committee and took considerable interest in it. He wrote a short history of the Newtyle library for the *Evening Telegraph* of 28 December 1956, to celebrate its centenary.

It became obvious that the library service was no longer sufficient for the needs of the day. Numbers of readers were dropping off—they had read all the books!! Also it was becoming increasingly difficult to get voluntary staff. On 5 January 1970 a branch of the Angus County Library was opened in the room of the Wharncliffe Hall locally known as the 'Armoury' because of its connection with the war-time Home Guard. This room was shelved and redecorated on its conversion to a library.

At the end of its life the funds of the library were handed over to the Newtyle Village Committee, who use it for financing the Local History Collection. The final Library Committee consisted of Messrs. James Fenwick, Hugh Hunter, and Bruce Johnstone.

So ended what could well be the last public subscription library in Scotland.

For a few years a small private subscription library was in operation at Graham Ballantine's shop about 1956.

Chapter 5

WORK

Agriculture [44 and 101]

The Rev. Small in the *Statistical Account* of 1792 gives 1,600 acres of arable land in the parish divided into 15 farms. The next fifty years saw advances in farming such that the acreage rose to 2,500 by 1815 [101—1842] then to about 3,000 acres by 1950.

In the 18th century farmers worked a rough four-fold rotation:

1. clover and rye-grass;
2. oats sown in March or April;
3. turnips, potatoes and pease sown in March or April (potato was food fit only for animals);
4. barley with grass sown in April or May.

Not much wheat was sown, but, if so, in September or October.

The farm worker had a long hard day. At seed-time he would rise at 5 a.m., dress his horse, clean the stables, feed them at 6.30, then get his own breakfast and start the day at 7 a.m. He came back to the farm at 11 to rest his horse, and do odd jobs, such as—tools to the smiddy; take unthreshed corn to the barn; or winnow corn. He fed the horse again at 1 p.m., himself at 2, and back to the fields to 6 p.m. Then feed and litter his horse, get his supper, and so to bed ('horse' could be one or a pair).

In summer he rose at 4 a.m., fed the horse with grass, and into the fields by 5 a.m. He had one hour for breakfast; and one hour for dinner between 1 and 2 p.m. The afternoon was spent hand-hoeing turnips or potatoes, or making hay, while the horse were in the fields regaling themselves on grass. He finished work about 9 p.m.

Food was mainly as much oatmeal in a wooden dish, as he thought he could eat. Boiling water was added until it thickened. This gruel was often used for the three meals. Sometimes, especially at harvest time, there would be pottage or porridge for breakfast with as much milk as he wished; for dinner a half loaf of bread (12 baked from 1 peck of coarse-milled flour) and three muchkins of small beer; for supper—the same as breakfast.

Reapers or shearers of corn may or may not be permanent workers on the farm, and usually were itinerant. They were 'well' paid at between 24 and 32 shillings plus food, in the Newtyle area. Women got between 16 and 24 shillings. Those with houses were given half a lippie (3½ lbs) of oatmeal for their supper. Shearing was often done by the piece—cutting down an acre was worth 7s to 8s. Each shearer got one shilling over and above his wages, or a share in a meal of beef and broth. At the end of the harvest there would be dancing and singing to the violin, and merrymaking. Then off the men would go, often after making an agreement with the farmer for next year's harvest.

Work in winter also went on from dawn to dusk, and even after. The horse were always attended to first—fed and dressed, stables cleaned, then the men could get breakfast. Work started about 8.30 a.m. for five hours— turn dung hills, clear drains and water courses, bundle straw, riddle or winnow grain, thresh grain, look after sheep and cattle, get supper ready for the horse, and get their own dinner at half past one. They started again at 2 and finished at 6 o'clock.

Some of the larger farms by the 1850s had threshing machines costing about £40 (Scots). Usually the threshing was done by hand by men called 'lotmen,' who received as pay the 25th boll of grain that they threshed out, with breakfast and dinner, or the 21st boll without victuals.

There were kilns for drying corn in some parishes of Angus but there is no indication of one in the Newtyle area. These varied in design often making use of a slope to get an upward draught. Some had one window, some three, and always with a doorway where the fire was lit. The windows, especially the one opposite the door, were high up and acted as ventilators, to carry the smoke away and not blacken the grain. Occasionally, if the draught was not very good, there would be a large bellows at the door with a long pipe bent up, in among the burning fuel. These kilns were usually built of stone and lime. Few of these existed in Angus in the latter half of the 18th century, and most of those that did, were near corn mills.

Some remnants of thirlage or feudalism remained at that time—tenants were directed to certain corn mills; ploughed and sowed the landlord's land (arriages); sheared or reaped his crop (bonnages); and carriages of various kinds. But these were fast disappearing by 1830 and being replaced by leasing.

Liming was a popular method of fertilising. It had been used as a cement in the parish of Craig in the latter half of the 18th century, and as a manure by Mr Scot of Dunninald in East Forfarshire. So much use was made of lime that it became an important trade—being brought by sea from the Firth of Forth and from Sunderland—the cheapest way. Two quarries existed in Forfarshire—one at Budden in Craig parish and the other at Stracathro.

The western part of Forfarshire was not rich in lime but a substitute was found in marl. About 1735 a Mr Pearson, owner of the estate of Balmadoes in Rescobie parish discovered marl in Balgavies loch. The marl was dragged or dredged from the bottom of the loch. By 1760 the Earl of Strathmore had Forfar loch drained, and the marl conveyed from it by means of a channel with locks. The best shell marl was found in Restennet loch in 1790. It was between two and thirteen feet deep and covered with a foot or two of moss. This served a double purpose because the moss was dried and used as fuel. Some marl was found in Newtyle parish but little or no indication of exactly where—the possibilities are the bogs at Ardler, Kirkinch, Nevay and Drumkilbo, and the mill and curling ponds. These ponds would not yield much marl.

Some farmers went to the extreme of putting as much marl on their fields as possible, thinking that this would produce more and better crops. The effect was exactly opposite, and many fields took years to recover. The habit that later became universal was to make a compost (that word *was* used in 1790) of earth, lime or marl, on the dunghill.

54

The first half of the 19th century saw a lot of draining and ploughing of pasture land to make it arable. Hatton Hill was ploughed almost to the top, and the land between Newtyle and Alyth Junction was drained. Where standing water, marsh and bog used to exist, now grew corn. There were considerable improvements made at Couston by Andrew Whitton. Lime and other materials were brought by rail from Dundee.

Farms were leased for 19 years. The chief grain crops were still oats and barley, but greater attention was being paid to rearing and feeding cattle and sheep. Some farmers were buying sheep-stock to eat off the winter turnips, then selling the fatted sheep in spring. Hugh Watson, who started the Aberdeen-Angus breed of cattle at Keillor, kept a permanent stock of Southdown sheep at Auchtertyre farm. There were 13 threshing mills in Newtyle parish by 1840 [101]—7 worked by horse, 5 by water and one at Auchtertyre by steam engine.

The 20th century saw the seven-fold rotation:

1. oats after a two-year ley;
2. potatoes getting the bulk of the farmyard manure, with 6 to 8 cwt of artificial manure per acre. Chiefly Majestic and King Edward for seed for the English market; Kerr's Pink and Golden Wonder as ware;
3. wheat sown in the latter half of November;
4. turnips and swedes, or partly sugar beet;
5. oats or barley with grass;
6. & 7. two-year ley.

Up to the 1914-18 war there was a tendency to depart from the strict succession of cropping, especially to leave the ley down for at least three years, and sometimes four. Between the wars this tendency increased and seemed to become very dependant on the state of the market, and its prospects, especially for barley.

Pre-1914 the main livestock (other than workhorse) were bullocks for fattening. The farmer reckoned on feeding in winter about three bullocks per acre of root crop, with oat straw, some hay later on, and about 4 to 8 lb of cake and other concentrates per head per day. In spring a further batch of store cattle were bought (a large percentage from Ireland) and fattened on grass.

Newtyle being near a town (Dundee) and some fair-sized concentrations of population, had a few dairy farms. Other than pedigree flocks of sheep—mainly Suffolks and Border Leicesters—there were no great flocks, because the ewes tend to get too fat, unless kept on the slopes of the Sidlaws. Lambs and tegs were bought in and fattened.

Kirkton farm up to and after the 1939-45 war had a number of pigs. Auchtertyre, Davidston and Denend farms kept hens, but not on a large scale. Each farm between the wars kept the small number of pigs on swill made from refuse and broke potatoes, and the hens would scrabble round the farmyard. The sale of eggs, butter and cheese surplus to their own requirements were pin money to the farmer's wife.

Hugh Watson

Hugh Watson was born on 4 October 1787 at Bannatyne House, Newtyle, where his father resided as factor to Belmont estate.

He had a short time at Edinburgh University, then in 1808, he leased Keillor farm and started to improve the polled cattle of the day. His father gave him six of his best cows and a bull (Tarnty Jock). Hugh went to Tarnty (or Trinity) Fair, Brechin, and bought ten of the blackest and best polled heifers and a bull. Earlier he had visited Robert Colling and studied his way of breeding shorthorns at first hand. He followed the same principle at Keillor—close breeding and good feeding. Each of his stock was succeeded in the herd by one of its sons.

He started exhibiting in local shows in 1810 and later swept the boards at the shows of the Highland and Agricultural Society. In 1828 he sent to Smithfield, London, a fat heifer of 130 to 140 stones 'with a fore-leg as fine as a roe-deer's,' which so delighted the Earl Spencer that he had a medal struck bearing her image. His ox was portrayed in Youatt's *Book of Cattle* as outstanding for the quality of meat and the amount of fat when slaughtered. At the Perth Show of 1829 all the exhibits of bulls and cows came from Keillor except one. At the 1836 Perth Show Hugh lifted first prize for an Angus bull; first and second for two Angus cows; and first for a 4-year-old Angus ox. In 1843 one of his oxen took first prize at the Highland Show in Dundee, after it had walked the 13 miles from Keillor the day before.

His cattle became known as the best in the country. Keillor supplied the first-class breeders with bulls. Hugh also acted as judge at International as well as British shows. His last show was at Aberdeen in 1858 where he exhibited an Aberdeen-Angus cow 'Old Grannie.' She had lived for 35 years, had had 25 calves, giving up breeding in her 29th year. After being killed by lightning, she was entered as No. 1 in the Aberdeen-Angus herd book.

James Thomson was the cattleman who looked after Old Grannie during her lifetime. He had been with Hugh Watson for 42 years. In 1858 he was presented with a medal and 100 francs by the Societie pour Protection des Animaux at the Aberdeen Show.

In 1860 the herd at Keillor was stricken with pleuro-pneumonia and was dispersed. This, and old age, must have influenced Hugh to leave Keillor. He moved to the Den of Perth and died there on 10 November 1865 aged 76. His wife, Margaret Rose, died a year later. The Aberdeen-Angus Cattle Society in 1965 had an inscription made on his gravestone in Newtyle Kirkyard to commemorate the centenary of his death.

William McCombie of Tillyfour continued Hugh's work so successfully that by 1870 the Aberdeen-Angus joined the beef Shorthorn and the Hereford as the world's leading beef herds.

As well as Keillor, Hugh Watson farmed Auchtertyre, Bannatyne Home Farm (now Kirkton) and Edderty. In the *Dundee, Perth and Cupar Advertiser* for 3 March 1837 he advertised that the house at Auchtertyre was to be let for one or more years. He would add a cow's keep and other conveniences, if required, all at a 'moderate rent.'

Hugh also bred Leicester and Southdown sheep—the Southdowns at Auchtertyre—and he is credited in the *Statistical Account* of 1842 as the one 'who first introduced the use of bone manure into this district of the county . . .'

He entered the social life of the county. He joined the Forfarshire Yeomanry. He entered a horse at Monifieth and Perth Race Meetings. He became friendly with Captain Barclay of Ury, and with him started the stage coach 'Defiant' between Aberdeen and Edinburgh. Sir Walter Scott was one of his friends.

Agricultural Contractors

This was unknown until roughly the 20th century. Some contracting went on in the early 1900s, but it was mainly carting. One can imagine the coal cart getting washed out, to cart lime, grain, straw, manure, or whatever, from farm to farm, or between the railhead at Newtyle and the farm. With the coming of the steam traction engine, contracting really started.

The greatest change came after the 1939-45 war. Various merchants, including Whitton of Meigle, rented fields from the farmers, then planted, harvested, graded and marketed potatoes.

John Easson developed a contracting business in Newtyle from about 1950 to 1970, using the old slaughterhouse area in the Glamis road as a base for his machines. In 1969 he had two combine-harvesters, two potato lifters, two balers, one turnip lifter, one rotovator, one potato-haulm pulveriser, two double ploughs, and four tractors; and employed three men.

Another contracting business based at Couston House was run by Alexander Findlay. It lasted about 4 years, when he emigrated to Australia. In 1967 he had one combine-harvester, two potato lifters, one baler, one turnip lifter, one pulveriser, one rotovator, three quadrupal ploughs, three tractors, three lime spreaders, and employed four men. He also used ammonia injectors and had three liquid ammonia tanks. This was a fairly new idea to inject anhydrous ammonia direct into the ground, but it did not seem to be very popular.

When Burnside quarry closed down in the early 1970s, the firm of R. W. & I. Steele of Millhole farm, leased the quarry to hold their agricultural equipment. Taking the quarry was a solution to one of their headaches. To enter Millhole farm one had to cross the old railway cutting by a bridge, which would deteriorate with the weight and vibration of heavy vehicles, and be too narrow for such as combine-harvesters. In 1967 they contracted out with tractors and lorries, mainly pulverising and spreading. They employed five men. They also worked Millhole farm.

Farm by Farm

In 1872 there were 20 farms and about 15 pendicles in Newtyle parish. By 1972 there were 11 farms and no pendicles.

Auchtertyre Farm

This was farmed up to about 1856 by Hugh Watson's father, and when he died in 1836 by Hugh himself. From 1856 for over 100 years it was farmed by the Bell family and 6 farm workers—grieve, cattleman, shepherd and three ploughmen.

In 1872 the farmhouse had three public rooms, kitchen, scullery, dairy and four bedrooms; with outhouses including a chaise-house, nag stable for three horse, and a loose-box.

The farm buildings consisted of a byre for 18 beasts with root house; a large barn with a thrashing machine worked by a fixed 8 horse-power vertical steam engine, and engine house and boiler house; two covered yards to hold 20 beasts with root house and loose-box; another byre for 8 beasts; four small yards with open sheds; boiling house, potato house; poultry house and cake house; large fodder house with granary over; loose-box; room for labourers and piggery.

The whole farm in 1872 covered about 970 acres; was supplied from spring water by gravitation; and was rented at £1,015 per year.

By 1967 Auchtertyre had taken in Crookston farm making it 1,160 acres, including 600 acres of hill. They had 600 Blackface x Leicester ewes; 30 black poll Aberdeen-Angus cattle for fattening; no pigs and 30 hens. There was also 4 acres of strawberries yielding between 2 and 4 tons for several years. The farm was operated by seven men, and had a grain-dryer and potato-lifter.

Bannatyne Home Farm

This farm was attached to Bannatyne House and up to 1868 the occupier of the house was also the farmer—no farm house. But Major Thomas seems to have agreed to the estate leasing the farm separately to John Millar.

In 1872 the farm house comprised two sitting rooms and three bedrooms, with kitchen, dairy and pantry. The farm buildings comprised stabling for five horse, with loft over; a cart shed, with granary over; boiling house, poultry house, loose-box, potato house, chaise house, and room for labourers; a barn with thrashing machine worked by water power; 4 byres with standing for 26 beasts; root house, fodder house, open shed and small yard. These buildings no longer exist, but there is still a mill-lade with wheel-pit close to Bannatyne House.

One point about the lease to John Millar in 1868 is that the proprietor kept the right to re-take a field just south of Bannatyne House, on six months' notice. This illustrates the importance the landlord gave to the mill, as this field contained the mill-pond and the lade. The farm occupied 130 acres.

In 1910 Kirkton farm house became a private home. The home farm and Kirkton farm merged, becoming the new Kirkton farm. The working of the home farm was likely taken on by Kirkton twenty years earlier, as the estate put their forester, Joseph Harbottle, into what was the Home farm house. The new Kirkton farm house was not built until 1908-10. The farm was worked by the farmer and one man.

Burnmouth Farm

From 1867 to 1886 this was farmed by David Soot who also farmed Templeton, Kinpurney and Edderty farms. He lived at Kinpurney. Burnmouth was held under a separate lease.

There was no farm-house as such in 1872, but there were seven cottages (two of them newly built in 1872). It covered just under 500 acres, and was worked by five men with another two in the bothy.

The farm buildings consisted of byres for 36 beasts, with gangways for feeding, and root and fodder houses; stables for 14 horse; a large barn combined with thrashing machinery, driven by an 18-foot water wheel (also used for pulping and chaff-cutting); wagon shed for 8 wagons, with granary over; nag stable (two stalls); two loose-boxes; boiling house, and two rooms for labourers; central open sheds in three ranges with feeding gangways; two large root houses and four enclosed yards; poultry house and manure house. The water wheel belonged to the landlord.

By 1967 Burnmouth had 450 acres all arable, and grew potatoes, wheat, barley, grass, hay and turnips. There were 200 Irish cattle and 300 sheep for feeding. The whole lot was worked by 8 men.

Burnside

This was a small farm or pendicle about a mile towards Dundee. By 1856 the land at Burnside and part of Newtyle Mill farm was tenanted by David Jamieson. It was taken over by Hatton in 1870. The last of the buildings were pulled down in the 1930s. From 1890 to 1897 the Parochial Board of Newtyle used one of the houses as a poorhouse.

Burnside is now part of Hatton and has completely lost any separate identity, except that the quarry bears its name.

Couston House and Farm

This belonged to Andrew Whitton, not the estate. The farm was run by three men, and the house had a gardener and coachman up to 1913—then a chauffeur till 1916. Andrew Whitton died in 1916.

From 1876 Henderston farm was worked with Couston. By 1930 Couston House was occupied by William L. Patullo, accountant, Meadowside, Dundee. The farm was worked by five men.

By 1967 there were 122 acres of arable land and 675 acres of hill (including Scotston hill). This supported about 1,100 sheep—Border Leicesters and Cheviots—with about 300 cattle, Highland x Aberdeen-Angus. The rotation of crops was—potatoes, barley, grass, hay and silage. It was worked by four men, with potatoes contracted out.

The farm had a small tree nursery for their own use.

Crookston Farm

This was one of the small farms or pendicles at Newbigging. For many years it has been included in Auchtertyre farm.

Davidston Farm

In the early 19th century this farm with Couston and Henderston was owned by the Presbytery of Dundee.

From 1856 to 1883 the mansion house and farm were owned by Patrick Millar of Balbeuchly and Robert Millar of Dollarbeg, Dollar. Then from 1883 to 1912 it was owned by Alexander Bell followed by Patrick Bell. After 1912 it was owned and worked by various people including from 1915 to 1920 by James Croll, nurseryman, Dundee. For most of the time it was worked by two men and the farmer.

By 1967 it covered 150 acres all arable, supporting about 45 cattle, 130 Cheviot sheep, 9 pigs and 40 Chafer 555 hens.

Denend Farm

In 1872 the farmhouse contained four rooms. The farm buildings were made up of two byres with standing for 18 beasts; root house and boiling house, poultry house, and small yard; wagon shed with granary over; barn with thrashing machine driven by water power; stable and open shed. There were two cottages and seven arable fields covering 88 acres. The rent was £238.

It was farmed in 1856-62 by Andrew Doig, and from then to 1914 by the Donaldsons, with two men, or one man and the farmer.

By 1967 the farm was still 88 acres, using a rotation of potatoes, wheat, grass (4 years), turnips and kale, and barley. The farmer kept 35 cows and heifers for milking; 15 for calving, and 25 under one and a half years old—Ayrshires and Friesians—producing about 60 gallons of milk per day, mostly sold locally. He had no bull but used artificial insemination. He had no sheep, but about 300 hens—Rhode Island Reds x Brown Leghorns. By the 1970s he had given up the hens.

Edderty Farm

This was a small hill farm included in Kinpurney farm from at least 1856 until 1887. In 1872 there were two cottages with farm premises of a 4-horse stable; barn; cattle byre; root house; open sheds and a yard.

From 1888 Edderty was used for grazing by Hatton farm and by 1900 was completely incorporated into Hatton, losing its independent identity and its buildings. One building was left as shelter for animals, and for some storage.

Hatton Farm

This was the toun or farm next to the Hall or Manor, the Castle of Newtyle.

One record of this farm is an advertisement in the *Dundee, Perth and Cupar Advertiser* for 3 March 1837, for a roup of fatstock at Hatton of Newtyle.

'To be sold on Tuesday 26 March, 30 stots, cows and queys and about 230 wethers.'

(A quey is a young cow that has not yet had a calf, i.e. a heifer).

60

In 1872 the farmhouse consisted of two sitting rooms; kitchen; store-room; wash house; dairy with cheese room; small room; water closet and five bedrooms. The farm premises were five byres with standing for 47 beasts; root house; fodder house; piggeries; chaise house; room for labourers; manure house; wagon and implement shed, with granary over; cake house with granary over; barn with thrashing machine driven by water; stable for 10 horse; loose box; yard and open sheds.

There were six cottages plus three at Burnside; 22 fields covering about 350 acres plus about 190 of hill. The rent was £650 per year.

By 1967 there were 300 cattle—Aberdeen-Angus x Hereford breeding herd, as well as about 950 sheep—Blackfaced and Border Leicesters. The farm was run by 8 men and the farmer.

From 1856 to the 1920s this was farmed by Charles Simpson (to 1877), then his son, Alex, until the 1920s with 4 to 5 men. From then until 1969 by Alexander Findlay followed by his son, James.

For about ten years from 1910 part of Hatton farm was used to grow fruit; operated by Watson and Langlands, then Langlands and Longair, fruit growers.

From 1871 Hatton included Burnside farm and pendicle, then from 1888 also Edderty farm.

Henderston Farm

From 1876 until the 1920s this farm was owned by Andrew Whitton, and worked in with Couston.

Keillor Farm

High Keillor and Hill of Keillor comprised in 1856 of four pendicles plus two cottages, reduced eventually by 1900 to one small farm.

The two were combined into High Keillor farm, and later into Keillor farm itself. From 1886 to 1906 there was a smiddy at Chapel of Keillor, run by James Fenwick, then his son, William. From 1907 this was occupied by farm servants when William Fenwick took over the Newtyle smiddy run by John Robertson.

Keillor farm was run by Hugh Watson (of Aberdeen-Angus fame) up to 1856, then up to 1912 by William Millar, followed by John Motion until the 1930s.

In 1872 Keillor had a fine house containing dining, drawing, and breakfast rooms; three smaller rooms; kitchen; small conservatory; pantry; water closet; 7 bedrooms; detached wash house; 2 small dairies; larder and laundry; nag stable for two horse; 3 loose boxes; harness room and carriage room.

The farm buildings (recently erected in 1872) comprised two byres with standing for 28 beasts; root house; another byre for ten beasts, with root house; covered yard with feeding gangway through the centre, and root house; another small byre; 2 rooms for labourers; large barn with thrashing machine driven by fixed steam engine; large lean-to straw shed; boiler and engine houses; coal house; potato house with loft over; stable for 14 horse; fodder house; two yards with open sheds; poultry house with implement shed; store room with loft over.

The threshing machine was formerly worked by water-power, and in 1872 the water wheel, though unused, was still there.

The farm covered about 800 acres, with 11 cottages. The rent was £1,420 per year.

Kinpurney Farm

This was farmed up to 1857 by David Waddell; then by David Soot up to 1885; by David McLaren up to 1898; Miss Harvey for five years, and taken over from 1904 to 1916 by Joseph G. Scott; and from then to the 1920s by A. H. Anderson & Son.

The farm house, erected in 1867, consisted of dining and drawing rooms; 2 small sitting rooms; kitchen; scullery, store room; dairy and two pantries; front and back staircases; three bedrooms, and servants' bedroom over the kitchen. The old farm house adjoining was used as wash-house and store room, with three rooms above and coal house.

The farm buildings consisted of byres for 38 beasts with feeding gang-ways, and large roothouse; barn with combined thrashing machine, driven by fixed vertical steam engine of 10 horse-power; engine and boiler house; stable for 14 horse; loose box with loft over; boiling house; wagon shed with granary over; room for labourers; open sheds with three yards, with feeding gangways and two roothouses; nag stable for three horse; harness room; carriage house with granary over; tool house and wood house.

The farm covered about 800 acres (500 arable), including Edderty and Templeton, and had 8 cottages at Kinpurney, 2 at Edderty and 4 at Templeton. The rent was £850 per year in 1872, but the landlord reserved the right to resume possession of the tower on Kinpurney Hill with 5 acres round it, if required at any time during the lease.

Templeton homestead consisted of farm house of 6 rooms with dairy and wood shed. The farm premises were made up of cart shed with granary over; byres for 20 beasts; stable for 7 horse; implement shed and two cottages.

By 1960 there were about 350 acres arable and 350 hill, with 200 cattle and 100 Leicester and Cheviot sheep. A rough rotation was worked—potatoes, wheat and barley, grass, turnips, cabbage and mangoes (2 acres), and silage (40-50 acres). Also grown was about 36 acres of raspberries. Six men were employed. One building, consisting of two houses, partly up the hill on the farm road to the quarry, was known as 'The Barracks'—built about 1910. This building was called 'The Barracks' because it housed the quarry workers.

Kirkton Farm

This was the toun or farm beside the kirk. It was originally sited on the Dundee road between the church and the Kettins road. The house in 1872 contained two sitting rooms; kitchen; store room; dairy; 3 bedrooms; wash house; coal house; etc. It is now a private house called Kirkton House.

The farm buildings comprised a stable for 5 horse, with sheaf loft over; barn with thrashing machine worked by horse-power byre; for 18 beasts; poultry house; boiling house; chaise house; cart shed with granary over; implement shed; 2 cattle sheds; and small yard. There was one cottage, and the whole farm covered about 140 acres.

By about 1890 Bannatyne home farm was incorporated, and that name was dropped. By 1910 the new Kirkton farm house was built on the home farm's ground, and the old Kirkton farm house was sold.

Sometime after 1930 Kirkton incorporated Pitnappie farm increasing the size to 380 acres with 54 acres of rough ground. The farmer in 1967 kept 60 breeding Irish cows; two black Aberdeen-Angus bulls; 130 sheep—Cheviot and Suffolk tups; and six pigs. He also grew raspberries at Pitnappie.

Millhole Farm

Sometime between 1817 and 1855 this was farmed by William Buttars.

In 1872 it was only a small farm of 110 acres, and the farmer, James Millar, lived in one of the two cottages. The farm buildings consisted of a byre for 16 beasts; root house; fodder house; stable for five horse; cart shed with granary over; small cattle shed; poultry house; open sheds with yard; barn with thrashing machine operated by water power; wood house; room for labourers. The rent was £155 per year.

In 1967 the farm had been increased by taking in part of Wester Pitnappie. The stock consisted of 45 heifers for calving, 50 Blackfaced and Leicester sheep, and 2 pigs. It was worked by 5 men, but they also contracted out, using tractors and lorries, doing mainly pulverising and lime-spreading. Since then the contracting has been extended.

In 1864 when the railway loop was built to cut out the Hatton incline, the company made a deep cutting between Millhole and the main road. A bridge was built over the cutting, but it is becoming unsuitable for present-day farm traffic.

Nethermill

This mill was located behind the Belmont Arms at Alyth Junction. It was the corn mill for the area. The Brown family were the millers from 1862 to 1914; first Thomas, senior, then Peter and Thomas, junior, then Peter himself. From 1900 to 1910 the owner was James Smith who also farmed Millhole. By the 1920s it was taken over by George and William Whittet.

Newbigging Farm

It was owned by the Moon family—from 1856 to 1884 by Alexander Moon, then William Moon till 1912. From then it was farmed by John Easson till 1916, and the Smith family till 1933 when it was incorporated into the Newtyle Bulb and Farming Co.

In 1872 the farm house had 5 rooms. The farm buildings consisted of a stable for 3 horse; 2 byres; a barn with thrashing machine worked by horse-power; cart shed; implement shed; open shed; boiling house; and covered about 60 acres.

Pitnappie Farm

There were originally two small farms here—Pitnappie and Wester Pitnappie. Part of Wester Pitnappie was incorporated in Millhole farm, and the small house used up to about 1960 as a farm cottage for Millhole. Then it was deserted.

Pitnappie itself by 1872 had a newly-built farm house of six rooms. The farm premises had 2 byres with standing for 21 beasts; 2 root houses; barn with thrashing machine worked by horse-power; wagon shed; calf house; boiling house; coal shed, with granary over; open shed and yard. The rent was £255 per year. It was later taken over by Kirkton farm.

Ralston Farm

This farm was started in 1911 by incorporating a number of Newbigging pendicles. It was farmed until 1929 by Donald Fleming, when it was taken over by Seymour Cobley Ltd., bulb growers, London. In 1933 it was worked by the newly-formed Newtyle Bulb and Farming Co.

Newtyle Bulb and Farming Co.

From 1913 an English bulb-growing firm (George Munro and, later, Seymour Cobley Ltd., 4 Tavistock Street, Covent Garden, London) rented some fields just north of Newtyle. It was run under a local manager—Mervyn E. H. Burnett.

In 1933 The Newtyle Bulb and Farming Co. was formed with Mervyn Burnett as chairman, and his son John as managing director. In 1967 the company had 16 men and 10 women on the permanent staff, and employed 60 women and school children at the height of the season. Their farms—Kirkton of Nevay, Newbigging and Ralston—covered 440 acres with 60 in bulbs. The rotation used was—bulbs (daffodils 2 years, and tulips 1 year); grain; grass/hay; two years grazing. This supported 100 Irish cattle. There was a quarter of an acre of glass, growing about 20 tons of daffodils for the early market. Gladioli were tried in summer, but they were uneconomic. The flowers were sent by rail all over Britain, and when the railway closed by 1963, the flowers were sent by road to Dundee and Perth (and even Glasgow) then the rest of the way by rail.

The bulbs and flowers were treated, sorted and packed in the old bone mill, and now the company uses the old railway station itself as a store, and for grading carrots.

Quarries

[41] 'At the head of Lundie Loch, and places adjacent, the Seedlay Hills exhibit perpendicular ledges of Whinstone rock, of great altitude, placed like mural crowns, upon their summits. These ledges are intersected by perpendicular fissures; and the spectator recognises an affectation of the imposing grandeur of columnar basalt. But they consist of rude blocks, which scale off, with softer matter interposed; and from their bases extend long sheets of alluvial whinstone soil, of great fertility.' (Headrick, 1813).

Along the slopes of the Sidlaws there were quite a number of quarries used mainly for stone for building; for roofing tyles; and later for making roads. The smallest of these quarries would have been used to build anything from a single cottage to a group of farm buildings, as long as the quarry was within reasonable cart-and-horse distance.

By 1872 there were five quarries in Newtyle parish:

1. Opposite Pitnappie road end, covering 0·4 acres. Out of use by 1872.
2. Pitnappie quarry, nearly opposite Davidston road end, covering 1·2 acres. Quarrying stopped by 1872, but it was used about 1940-60 as a dump for village refuse. Some of the 19th century buildings in Dundee are recorded as having been built with stone from this quarry.
3. Auchtertyre quarry, near the entrance to the present Kinpurnie Castle, covered 0·4 acres. Tennis courts were built in it. This was a small quarry and out of use by 1872.
4. Millhole quarry was one of reasonable size—1·1 acres. It was used by the Road Trustees in 1872 for road metal.
5. Kinpurney quarry (on the farm road up the hill) covered nearly 4 acres, and was out of use by 1872. The stone from it was used to build many of the houses in Newtyle including the old school in North Street.

The largest quarry at Burnside on the Dundee road was not developed until about 1883, when it was opened up by James Mann for road metalling. On James' death the business was carried on by his three sons—William, David and John. (William was still alive in the 1930s). John seems to have been the quarry master. He and his two brothers, like their father, worked with pick and shovel, two carts and horse. They quarried and carted the metal to the roadside, where they broke it up. By 1902 they employed another two men—John Tulloch and John McDonald.

By the 1930s John Gray and Sons, the Newtyle masons, took over the business. They crushed and graded the rock using a traction engine as motive power. In the 1940s they sold out to William Briggs of Dundee, who employed about 30 men blasting, crushing, grading and tarring. By 1967 the quarry was producing 116,000 tons per year. The hole became so big that they began to encroach on the right-of-way called 'Aggiesidie,' which led from Sunnyhall at Lundie Loch to Newtyle. Briggs applied for and got permission, to re-align this right-of-way.

Briggs also had a vehicle maintenance and garage at the corner of Church Street and Commercial Street. Many of the drivers stayed in the village, along with some who worked at Castlehill Sand Quarry near Blairgowrie, also owned by Briggs.

In the 1960s Briggs was incorporated in a larger group of companies. When the lease ran out by 1970, it was not renewed. The Burnside quarry closed down.

It is now occupied by the Steeles of Millhole, agricultural contractors, who use it to store their machines. The weigh-bridge still stands on the Dundee road at the entrance to the quarry.

32-loom factory and drying loft built by George Moon about 1850.
Used as such till about 1880. Locally known as the 'Jam Factory.'

Belmont Street. 16 cottages to house George Moon's weavers.
Consisted of 2-roomed and 1-roomed houses and attics.

Linen

In the 18th century flax was included in the four-fold rotation of crops in Angus and Fife. Weavers from Newtyle parish have been recorded as fighting for Prince Charlie at Culloden in 1746 [59].

Perhaps a resume of the linen industry may help to replace the scarcity of local information.

The flax of commerce is *Linum usitatissum*—the common flax, growing 1½ to 2 feet high, with pale blue flowers. It is distinguished from the garden linum by having broader leaves; mostly single stem instead of several from the same root; and it is taller.

The plant was reaped or pulled; dried and then thashed to separate out the seed. The seed is pressed to extract the oil—lin(t)seed oil—and the residue was made into oil-cake for cattle food. This was the process carried out by the 'Chemical Works' or 'Bone Mill' at Newtyle.

The stems were retted in water—usually in ponds or pits. but sometimes in stone troughs about 4ft long, 2ft wide and 2ft deep. This process took several weeks and gave off an offensive smell. The burns or streams must have been polluted very badly, because even in the 17th century bye-laws were passed in some places, as to the use of troughs, or where retting was to be done. The only possible relic of this process could be the troughs; and none, to my knowledge, have been found in Newtyle parish.

After retting the flax stems were tied into bundles, dried and scutched. Scutching or beating produces long fibres (called line) for spinning, and some very short, broken fibres (called tow). About 1750 scutching mills worked by water wheels came into use in Scotland.

The next process was hackling to separate the line and tow. Both were spun, but the line produced the best quality linen.

Tow-guns were a popular toy in the late 18th and early 19th centuries. A wad of tow—usually waste tow called 'pob'—was rammed into the end of a tube fairly tightly, then it was forced out by blowing hard. The more sophisticated had a plunger. These guns could be made by anyone with time and patience (and there was plenty of both). Pick a straight twig, half an inch or more in diameter, any reasonable length (say 6 to 10 inches), but without any branches, from the growing tree (rowan or mountain ash was the commonest). This is soaked, beaten and rolled on the knee, until the bark can be slipped off as a tube. A plunger can be made with a half to one inch of the solid core, inserted in the tube, and pushed with a thinner twig. This toy was later replaced by the potato gun.

The cloth woven was a coarse linen called 'ticking,' or Osnaburg or Osenburg (from Osnaburg in Germany).

When the new planned villages were being formed (c1780 to 1840) linen was one of the main rural industries [51]. It became reasonably profitable for the new villagers. So landlords saw an opportunity to lay out capital to get a maximum of rent, and heighten the value of the land. Other factors were responsible for laying out the new village of Newtyle—the railway to Dundee; the mechanisation of the textile industry in Dundee (e.g. Cox's mill in Lochee); and the general decline of hand-loom weaving. The Lochee weavers saw a more independent life in the rural village, so many came to Newtyle.

LOOMSHOPS.

This row of two-storey houses was originally 5 two-roomed houses with 5 loom-shops on the lower floor, each holding 4 looms. . Now two houses—Nos. 25 and 27 North Street. The lower house to the left was the schoolhouse.

No. 35 North Street. Built about 1856. Then occupied by Andrew Fitchie, weaver. The part on the right with the small windows was a 4-loom shop.
On left (part only shown)—No. 37/39 was built in 1870. Occupied by George Corbett Dingwall, retired gardener, from 1881 to 1903. He called it 'Achterneed.'

Most village markets were where cloth, yarn and flax were sold, but Newtyle was too new to have a market. The older neighbouring village of Meigle had its square where its market was held—on Tuesdays. Most of the sales from Newtyle would be made in Dundee, which meant a long slow trek along the 'road and the miles tae Dundee.' And what a road!—a winding, twisting muddy or dusty cart track—up at dawn, a journey of three or four hours each way, and home at dusk, or after! The railway must have been a great help—at increased cost.

Some planned villages did not come off, e.g. Mr Nairne of Drumkilbo planned Kirkinch as a manufacturing village in 1838. In planning Newtyle the Earl of Wharncliffe was given astute and far-sighted advice by his factor, Andrew Dalgairns of Ingliston [51 and 117].

Others saw their chance. Out of a large family called Moon, one farmed Newbigging, one became a minister in Dundee, and George became a linen manufacturer in Newtyle. He feued the ground between Church Street and Belmont Street, and built a factory and warehouse (later known as the 'jam factory'), along with 16 houses as a terrace in Belmont Street. The factory could house 32 looms with the loft above for drying and as a warehouse. Weaving was paid for by the piece. Moon would allow for rent of a house and loom-shop, and probably hire of loom. So wages would be low.

George's father, John, was already a manufacturer as well as farmer at Newbigging. He died in 1833 aged 61.

Advertisements in the *Dundee, Perth and Cupar Advertiser* were directed at weavers—houses and loom-shops:

1. 30 October 1835. 'A number of dwelling houses and weaving-shops. Apply to J. and R. Ower, west end of Hawkhill, Dundee, or to Colquhon Stewart in Newtyle.'

2. 3 March 1837. 'Several houses and gardens to let. Weavers preferred. Apply to George Moon.'
   (This is possibly a 10-loom factory at the corner of Church Street and Castle Street, now occupied by houses and a grocer's shop).

3. 2 August 1839. 'In North Street consisting of—
   (a) cottage of one story and attics
       (the old school house);
   (b) tenement of two stories, with 5 weaving shops on the ground floor, each with four loom stances (now two houses);
   (c) tenement of two stories—weaving shop and house
       (demolished and replaced by modern old folks' houses).

The following count of looms in Newtyle can only be an estimate—or more likely, an underestimate. They do not include those in Newbigging and other places in the parish. The figures are for the village only, and include the two factories as two loom-shops:

c1840—117 looms (this *may* include Newbigging)

1856—	97 looms	14 loom-shops
1867—	64 looms	10 loom-shops
1871-7—	47 looms	5 loom-shops.

I have found no further mention of looms or loom-shops after this date [110]. The 32-loom factory was used by William Moon, Newbigging, as a grain loft, and the 10-loom factory was empty.

The Bone Mill or Chemical Works was conveniently built at the terminal of the railway, possibly between 1834 and 1837. It was advertised as a flax and bone mill for sale in the *Dundee, Perth and Cupar Advertiser* on 3 March 1837. This gives as the owner James Murison, and states 'the whole buildings have recently been erected.' These consisted of engine-house and bone mill ready for use, with some driving machinery put into the flax mill; a counting house; stable other buildings. The print in Gershwin Cumming's *Forfarshire Illustrated* of 1848 [27] shows this as a smallish group of buildings.

It was leased by David Hill of Bannatyne House. There is an inscription on the wall of the mill above what had been a door—D.H.1856. We can assume that David Hill built an extension and completed the flax mill. He is also recorded as being a coal and lime merchant.

David Hill sold out to Captain (or Major) Thomas by 1862. Thomas died in 1880, when the business was carried on by James Soutar as manager under trusteeship for two years. It was then taken over by Thomas Soutar, manure manufacturers, Blairgowrie, until 1891, when the Newtyle Chemical Co. was formed with John Henry as manager.

In December 1911 it was closed down. From then onwards the 'Bone Mill' was used as a conglomerate of stores by various people—Robert Henry, manure agent; James Clark, plumber, Coupar Angus; Alexander Crichton, slater, Meigle; and a store and stable for George Munro, 4 Tavistock Street, London. Hearsay has German prisoners-of-war housed there during 1914-18.

Right up to the 1930s the buildings were still being used as various stores although the occupants changed—the stable and store by Seymour Cobley Ltd., bulb growers, 4 Tavistock Street, London; store by Mervyn E. H. Burnett (Cobley's manager); and store by John Walton, plumber. Gradually it was all taken over by the Newtyle Bulb and Farming Co.

Gas Works

A small gas works was established by David Hill of Bannatyne House in 1855 at the 'Bone Mill.' This supplied coal gas to the mill itself, and other buildings in the village. Major Thomas of Bannatyne and Thomas Soutar of Blairgowrie continued the supply along with the mill. By the time the Newtyle Chemical Co. was formed in 1891, the gas works were closed down.

Gas light had been put into Newtyle school in 1874, and even yet some of the lead gas piping can be found in some older houses in the village.

Jam Factory

Watson and Lumgair, Dundee, started to use Moon's old 32-loom factory to make jam. There is a record of a William Cochrane, jam factory worker, living in Church Street in 1911 [110]. Jam-making ceased about 1929 when the building was used as a variety of stores.

Distilling

The distillery at Nevay was owned and run by Alexander Waddell of Nevay Farm (the present East Nevay farm). Alex died and David, his son, farmer at Templeton, was trustee for the family. He advertised in the *Dundee, Perth and Cupar Advertiser* on 8 April 1836, for the sale of the distilling utensils. This included two coppers, one containing 1,100 gallons and the other about 700.

The remainder of the utensils were put up at a public roup at East Nevay on Tuesday 22 May 1838 (*Dundee, Perth and Cupar Advertiser*, 11 and 18 May 1838). These consisted of tuns, coolers, stone steeps, excise locks, etc., and the malt kiln bedding of tile along with fire-bricks.

There are still the 'distillery wells' on the farm, but no water from them.

Mills

The Mill of Newtyle and Balmaw was situated at the east end of South Street, now occupied by two houses—Milton and Burnbank.

The mill was operated by a water wheel, with a lade (the burn) from the pond now in Dalnaglack grounds. In the 17th and 18th centuries Barons' Courts were held here.

James Burman was born there on 2 May 1777, became the miller and died there on 22 December 1859. His son, David Clark Burman, was born there on 7 February 1830. He became a master mariner, and when he retired he returned to the village of his birth. He built the 'Anchorage' at the corner of Castle Street and Belmont Street. The top room was built like the bridge of a ship, and he had a flagpole. He died there on 11 July 1906, and was buried in Dundee.

From 1845 to 1876 James Saunders operated this mill as a sawmill. He used a water wheel 14ft in diameter. From 1876 to 1896 it was occupied by D. Cardean. It is uncertain whether he just occupied the house or ran the sawmill [79].

According to the *New Statistical Account* of 1842 [101] there were two meal-mills and two saw-mills in Newtyle parish.

The School Management Committee's minutes record the saw-mill as closing down in October 1929 [79]. It may have operated separately from 'Milton House.'

Chapter 6

TRANSPORT

The Dundee and Newtyle Railway

[References—13; 32; 34; 50; 54; 56; 88; 90; 102; 114; 118; 120; 125].

Early railways were used in quarries, mines, works and factories. They were drawn by men (or women or children) or horse.

By 1802 Trevithick's steam road locomotive was invented, and two years later he produced a steam rail locomotive for the Pennydarren Iron Works near Merthyr Tydfil. In the same year (1804) the Surrey Iron Railway was running from Wandsworth to Croydon—drawn by horse. In 1806 the Oystermouth Railway from Swansea to Oystermouth carried passengers and was drawn by horse.

George Stephenson built his Killingworth colliery locomotive in 1815, and 'Locomotive No. 1' in 1825 for the Stockton and Darlington Railway. His engine 'The Rocket' ran in the trials for the Liverpool and Manchester Railway in 1829.

Up to 1825 thoughts were turning to a link between Dundee and Strathmore 'for the expeditious and economical conveyance of merchandise, grain, and all descriptions of farm produce; and of manure, stones, lime, coal, and other heavy and bulky articles' (Prospectus 1825). Possibly the survey carried out by Robert Stephenson in 1810 for a canal from Arbroath to Forfar, and then to Perth, and its rejection in 1825, had egged on the Dundee business men to build the railway.

On 1 February 1825, a meeting of subscribers for the survey of a railway between Dundee and Strathmore, was held in Dundee with George Kinloch of Kinloch in the chair. A committee was elected—the only Newtyle person on it being William Watson of Auchtertyre [106].

Charles Landale was asked to prepare a survey. He recommended using horse to pull the wagons along the level stretches, but reported that 'in the long term there is reason for believing that machines will work at much less expense than horses.' He knew that no satisfactory locomotive had been produced, but that it was a mechanical perfection that was sure to come.

The Carmichael brothers of Dundee contracted to produce the three stationary engines for £3,700 [56], and Landale estimated the whole cost not to exceed £26,000. This capital was subscribed; the largest shareholders being the town of Dundee, the Earl of Airlie, Lord Wharncliffe, the Rt. Hon. William Ogilvie, and George Kinloch; each subscribing £1,000. George Kinloch acted as chairman.

Kinloch and Landale went up to London in April 1826 to pilot the Railway Bill through Parliament [106]. The Dundee and Newtyle Railway Act was passed on 26 May 1826.

Railway Station at Newtyle.

First Railway Engine in Scotland, 1833
Dundee & Newtyle Railway

From 1825 to 1831 there were frequent entries in Mrs Kinloch's diary—'Mr K. went to a railway meeting' [106]. Her husband took a keen interest in, and spent a lot of time with, the railway.

The line was eventually opened on 16 December 1831 at a cost which greatly exceeded the original estimate. The first carriages were two old stage coaches, one called 'Tally-ho,' fitted with wheels to suit the rails [132]. According to Mrs Kinloch's diary the railway seemed to pay dividends in its early years. Coaches connected the railway station at Newtyle with Coupar Angus and Blairgowrie.

Tennant in his book [106] notes that a letter dated 28 May 1832 from 'Cousin Rebecca' to 'Dear Emily' had been found. It is worth quoting:

'You can't think how delighted I was last week with the ride from Dundee to Newtyle in the Railway Coach. The bustle at taking my seat—by-the-by neat ladders should be furnished by which to ascend the coach instead of compelling the ladies to scramble up by long strides, and coming off the coach is worse for one's petticoats are entangled, and the inconvenience is so bad as you can't imagine. Well, as I was saying, the bustle, the tolling of the Railway Bell, the sudden movement of sixty human beings by an unseen power upwards like a flock of geese in the air, and onwards by a horse at full gallop—the light and shade of the tunnel through the Law—by the by it's rather dark about the centre; however that depends upon who one happens to be seated beside—the promiscuous mixture of young lassies, young ladies and crones—dandies, parsons, farmers, merchants, weavers and ploughmen—the varied expression of faces, some merry, some stupid, some sad—the driver Sam lauding the merits of his horse and cracking his whip and his jokes. Dundee and its foul-mouthed chimney stalks fading from our view—flying through the mountainous region, the atmosphere which is cool as the Arctic regions—the sudden bursting on us of the warm rich vale of Strathmore—all contributed to my amusement. After passing through the tunnel, a dandy waved his hand indicating his intention to take a seat—in his hand a fishing rod and in his cheek a cigar. He tript lightly to his seat and, though snug himself, annoyed me with the fumes of his tobacco. A labourer sat behind him with a cutty pipe stuffed with pigtail. The smoke and smell was almost insufferable and I was almost choked. I would complain to Mr Kinloch but he is such an advocate for the liberty of the subject that I have little hope by his means of putting an end to the filthy practice. Little did the dandy know that, but for his nasty cigar, I could have admired him.   Your cousin, Rebecca.'

The Glasgow to Gurnkirk Railway was opened a few months before the Dundee and Newtyle Railway. It was mainly freight, so the 'Kinloch' Railway may well be the first passenger railway in Scotland.

George Kinloch died before steam engines operated on the railway, and he was never able to push his other interest—the new town of Washington at Ardler.

As made, the Dundee/Newtyle railway included three inclined planes worked by stationary engines and ropes:

(a) Law incline, Dundee—1.060 yards long with a gradient of 1 in 10.

(b) Balbeuchly incline—1,700 yards long with a gradient of 1 in 25.

(c) Hatton incline, Newtyle—1,000 yards long with a gradient of 1 in 13.

Only the Law incline had a passing place, the others were single track throughout. In 1843 the three stationary engines consumed 85 tons of coal per month—mostly from Preston Grange Colliery, east of Edinburgh—at a cost of 10/- per ton delivered. The gauge was 4ft 6½in.

The Newtyle and Coupar Angus Railway Act was passed on 21 July 1835, and the line was opened in February 1837. Up to then stage coaches were run between Coupar and Newtyle meeting the trains.

An advertisement appeared in the *Dundee, Perth and Cupar Advertiser* for 3 March 1837:

'Coupar Angus and Newtyle Railway.

The COACHES on this Railway will commence running THREE DAYS A-WEEK, upon Friday first, the 24th instant, as follows until further notice:
Upon Tuesdays and Saturdays

From Coupar Angus: leaving the present termination there at seven o'clock a.m.

From Newtyle: immediately on arrival there of the last Railway Coach from Dundee in the afternoon.

Upon Fridays only

From Coupar Angus: leaving the present termination there at seven o'clock a.m., and a quarter before ten o'clock a.m.

From Newtyle at eight o'clock a.m. and immediately on arrival there of the last Railway Coach from Dundee in the afternoon.

The fares to be as under:

First Class Coach from Coupar to Newtyle	–	9d each
Half-way	–	4d
Second Class Coach from Coupar to Newtyle	–	6d each
Half-way	–	3d

Coupar Angus. February 20, 1837.'

The Newtyle and Glamiss Railway Act was passed on 30 July 1833 but its opening does not appear to be confirmed. An advertisement in the *Dundee Advertiser* of 2 August 1839, gives the running times of the 'TRAINS OF COACHES' from Dundee to Newtyle, Coupar Angus and Glammis. (Note the spellings of Glamis). They started from Dundee and from Newtyle at 8 a.m.; 11 a.m.; and 6.30 p.m.—two trains simultaneously—so some passing places were available by that time. It gives the times from Coupar Angus but none from Glammis, beyond stating 'Omnibus between Glammis, Kirriemuir and Forfar.' This started on Wednesday 31 July 1839 between the railway depots and met the trains. It is possible that no train ran between Newtyle and Glamis, although the embankment can still be seen near Nethermill at Alyth Junction, behind the hotel.

The same advertisement also states:

'Railway-passengers taken up or set down at the following places only—

x DUNDEE
   Offset at back of Law.
x Ditto at the Flour Depot, St Mary's Road.
x Ditto at Baldragon Depot.
   Foot of Balbeuchly incline.
x Offset at Auchterhouse Depot.

x NEWTYLE—	x NEWTYLE—
Washington.	x Kirkinch.
x Ardler Depot.	Leason Hill.
x COUPAR ANGUS.	x Eassie.
	x GLAMMIS.'

Some of those stops (those marked x) appeared to have buildings, and the others were simply halts or crossings, or some convenient place to allow passengers on or off.

On 30 March 1838 Mr Nairne of Drumkilbo advertised feus at Kirkinch to form a manufacturing village, emphasising the nearness of the railway. But this was cancelled shortly after.

Goods trains were started at each end of the Dundee and Newtyle Railway at 6 a.m.; 1 p.m.; and 4.30 p.m. It seems that these were 'thorough' trains which could take a limited load so 'linens, yarns and flax will have the preference.' (*Advertiser*, 2 August 1839).

By 1838 the Company was in trouble. A meeting was called at the Depot at Hospital Ward, Dundee, on 10 April, for the purpose 'of considering articles of roup prepared by the Committee for a lease of the Railway: (for) receiving the resignation of such members as may wish to decline continuing in the Committee, and, if the meeting sees fit, appointing others: or, if the meeting think it more desirable, appointing *DIRECTORS* to manage the affairs of the Company.'

By the Act of 27 July 1846 the Dundee and Perth Railway Company were empowered to purchase the Dundee and Newtyle Railway. But the arrangement, in the end, was for a lease to the Dundee and Perth.

The Dundee and Newtyle Railway Act of 2 July 1847 authorised:

(1) The alteration of the gauge from 4ft 6½in to the standard gauge of 4ft 8½in. This was done on the Dundee/Newtyle, Newtyle/Glammis and Newtyle/Coupar Angus railways simultaneously.

(2) The opening out of the tunnel through the Law.
   (This was never done).

(3) The deviation of the line from the Dichty Water to Auchterhouse, cutting out the Balbeuchly incline.
   (This was carried out in 1859).

The way was now clear for the Dundee and Perth Company to plan the join-up of the Dundee/Newtyle line with the Dundee/Perth railway. This was authorised by the Dundee and Newtyle Railway Act of 21 July 1859. The new combine—the Dundee and Perth and Aberdeen Railway Junction Company—started to cut out the stationary engines (they had been running for over 20 years). They carried out two deviations:

(a) from Rosemill to Auchterhouse cutting out the Balbeuchly incline and station, and building new stations at Dronley and Auchterhouse. This was opened on 1 November 1860;

(b) the Lochee deviation was opened on 10 June 1861. The Law incline and the Dundee terminus in Ward Road were closed. New stations were opened at Lochee, Victoria and Liff. (Lochee West—previously Camperdown and Victoria—was closed in 1917).

In 1863 the Scottish Central Railway Company took over the Dundee and Perth and Aberdeen Junction Co., making them the lessees of the Dundee and Newtyle Railway.

On the Strathmore side of Newtyle, the Scottish Midland Junction Railway was formed under its Act of 1845. The traffic was first worked from Perth through Coupar Angus to Meigle Junction station. This station was opened about 1857-60 and was there before the Alyth Branch line was made. After the Alyth Branch was opened, the name Meigle Junction was changed to Alyth Junction (1 November 1876). Also on that date the name of Fullarton station on the Alyth Branch was changed to Meigle.

The Scottish Central Railway Act of 24 July 1864 authorised that company to make a deviation from Pitnappie to Newtyle, cutting out the last of the three inclines—Hatton. So the large loop was formed, and a new station built at Newtyle. The Act also provided for the Scottish North-Eastern Company (who took over from the Scottish Central) sharing the cost of the work and the joint station at Newtyle. The same Act also authorised the making of a new line from the new station at Newtyle to connect with the former Newtyle and Coupar Angus Railway, and with the main line to the north at Meigle Junction. Some of this was not carried out until the Caledonian took over.

The Caledonian Railway Company took over the Scottish Central in 1865, and the Scottish North-Eastern in 1867. By the Caledonian Railway Act of 1867, the Company was authorised to connect the line from the old Newtyle station to Meigle Junction (opened 3 August 1868). The Cale (as it was familiarily known) used the old Newtyle station as a goods station; and during their lifetime they must have closed the old booking-office and workshop situated across Commercial Street from the station. They must also have built the turn-table situated at the north corner of the public park.

The establishment in 1840 included:

1 man and a horse for the top of the Law incline.

    1 man and a horse for the top of the Balbeuchly incline.

    2 locomotive drivers, 2 firemen, 2 trainmen, 2 guards.

        (Replacing the horse).

1 policeman for the Dundee incline.

The manager had a salary of £70 per year.

Up to the end of the century there was a complement of between 10 and 15 railway workers, plus a stationmaster, at the Newtyle end. In addition there was a stationmaster and 5 to 6 men employed at Alyth Junction.

Other than some hints at the beginning of some success, the Dundee and Newtyle Railway never really paid its way. For a period (not dated) the operating costs averaged $83\frac{1}{2}\%$. This was too high, as it left $16\frac{1}{2}\%$ towards distribution—capital, dividend, interest on loans, etc. If we consider the number of men to operate the three inclines, then the operating costs could be nothing else but high.

The two level stretches were worked by wagon and horse until September 1833. There have been ideas about using sails and one early drawing in a newspaper (*Weekly News*, 5 November 1898) has a coach going merrily along the Newtyle to Coupar Angus line under sail (the horse running free behind it) at a good 20 mph with a strong wind. It's a nice idea—attributed to the horse-driver William Whitelaw. It is doubtful if even on a stormy day there would be enough force to overcome the frictions of wheels and axles—and the wind in the right direction.

George Duncan, 4th Earl of Camperdown [125], in his memoirs says 'One of my old men at the Lambeth Engine Works showed me a very old newspaper cutting describing the working of the Dundee and Newtyle by horses from Hatton Castle to Balbeuchly. The 'Newtyle gap' in the Sidlaws acts like a funnel to the wind when blowing from NW to SW which no doubt suggested the use of a sail on one of the wagons which with a favourable wind would greatly assist the horse haulage. They found that sometimes the wind power could outstrip the horse haul altogether which led to quite a curious scheme whereby the horse could be carried onwards as a passenger until he was needed. This was accomplished by having, at the back of the wagon, which carried the sail, a flap which let down to the rail level—on this flap the horse mounted in the rear and remained inside the box wagon until he was needed . . . I do not think that the scheme could have been successfully carried out in the open between the foot of Balbeuchly Bank and the winding engine on Dundee Law.'

George wrote his memoirs between 1900 and 1918, when he was about 60 years old, and was writing from memory, after a lifetime in America as an engineer, and interested in railways.

In September 1833 Messrs. Carmichael of Dundee made the first locomotive [34 & 56], the 'Earl of Wharncliffe,' and later a second named the 'Earl of Airlie.' The engines cost £700 each plus £30 for the tender. They lasted about 30 years. To quote from a newspaper cutting of somewhere between 1870 and 1880:

> 'As might be supposed the starting of the first locomotive on the first railway in Scotland was regarded as one of the greatest wonders of the day, and thousands turned out to see it. To test the power of the engine, 20 wagons each laden with six tons of coal, were placed in a line in order to be drawn. There was rapt attention until something was put in proper order, and the locomotive engine moved off with its great load with comparative ease amidst the hearty cheers of the spectators, who appeared delighted at the wonderful achievement.'

In March 1834 a third engine was built by the Dundee Foundry Co. for £700. It was never named but was known as the 'Trotter' to staff and passengers.

A fourth engine of the Planet class was purchased in April 1836 from Robert Stephenson & Co. It was known as 'The John Bull.' Its total cost including tender, spare parts, freight and insurance (by sea from Newcastle) was over £1,150.

The railway line was 'mainly single-track of wrought-iron 'fish-bellied' rails made by Longridge & Co. of Bedlington, Durham—about 28 lb to the foot, set in cast-iron chairs pinned to freestone blocks which acted as sleepers.' (Lythe—*Evening Telegraph*, 23-25 October 1951). An example of a fish-belly rail was found at Newtyle and kept there.

There have been a number of accidents on the line—even when building the Law tunnel, there were roof collapses with fatal results. Ropes on the inclines were another source of fatal and not-so-fatal results. We find in September 1838 that David Powrie was paid £1 3s 6d for making a coffin for William Carr killed on the Hatton incline [90].

Some of these accidents were not without humour and one example was Auld Jess, a local character. It was the custom at the end of the century to take the train on a Friday morning to Dundee for the market, to sell produce and return in the evening with groceries, etc. Coming back to Newtyle one day the rope broke half-way down the Hatton incline, the coach hit the buffers and fell over on its side. Jess's remarks were reputed to be— 'My! My! it was a gran' fest hurl doon the brae, bit the open kerridges stoppit ower quick. We wir a' coupit oot on tae the girse amon' oor parcels an' groceries. Maist o' us were seek wi' the fricht, bit a drap o' brandy oot o' a bottle frae the hotel worked the oracle. Eh, sirs, bit ma airms an' legs dirled for near a week efter.' [44]. (The story may be true or it may have legs on it. Anyway it's a good one).

The following is a list of stationmasters at Newtyle:

Mr Buttar	about 1836 to 1857
John Henry	1857-1860
W. Gibson	1860-7
A. Philip	1867-8 (Inspector of Railway)
John Birse	1876-86
David Johnston	1886-1928
Charles Davidson	1929- ?

Rabbie Anderson was gatekeeper at the level crossing on the Eassie road for many years. He had a small hut at the crossing. His duties were to open and close the gates when necessary, and tend the lamps. He was well-known in his Cale uniform, and the characteristic cap with C.R. on it.

The London Midland and Scottish Railway Co. took over the Cale in 1923, and subsequently British Rail on 1 January 1948.

Trains were running direct from Dundee to Blairgowrie. Those with a non-stop or limited stop were known as the 'Blairgowrie Express'; the slower one was called the 'Blairie'; and the train from Alyth Junction to Alyth was the 'Trappie.' Many a joke was told about the Blairie, as it chugged up the incline from Newtyle south to Dundee, through the cutting known as the 'Gullet.' One was supposed to be able to jump out of one's carriage, pick some flowers, and jump back into the same carriage again.

At the Dundee end it was known to have just missed the Blair train at the West station, then catch a tramcar to Downfield, beating the train on its long journey round by Ninewells, Liff and Lochee, and all the stops therein.

One memorable occasion was in 1948 when there was a smash near Ardler. The local from Newtyle to Coupar Angus had to drive along the main Perth-Aberdeen line for a short distance. Just as the local entered that short stretch, the Aberdeen express hit it. The driver of the local, John Laing, was killed.

On the 8th January 1955 the Blairie ran for the last time, driven by James Robertson, 3 Gibson Terrace, Dundee, and the fireman was Alex Barclay, 4 McVicar's Lane, Lochee. There was some fun that night—fog detonators on the line at every station; people dressed in mourning; streamers; hooting train whistles; and so on.

Goods trains ran up to November 1964, but finally the line was closed and the track lifted, bridges taken down, etc. For some time the line from Dundee near Kirkton farm was used as a storage for wagons awaiting breaking up. They eventually disappeared.

The Blairie ran once more on 20 May 1961 for railway enthusiasts. It was supposed to have been drawn by a 40-year-old Pickersgill engine. Something went wrong and it was pulled by a diesel.

David Lamond (*Dundee Courier*, 28 February 1903)

Mr and Mrs Lamond were married on 23 February 1839 by the Rev. James Ramsay of Alyth. His wife, Janet Anderson, was born in Alyth, and David was born in Newtyle. He was employed as a corn miller at a mill near Ardler. He later worked as fireman on the stationary engine at Hatton Hill, and in 1849 he became fireman on the 'Earl of Airlie,' one of the first locomotives on the Dundee-Newtyle railway. After a few years as fireman he was promoted to driver of the same engine, working between Hatton and Balbeuchly, a distance of $4\frac{1}{2}$ miles. The engine, carriages and wagons were light. Each wagon could not take more than two tons. The passenger carriages were 'wretched conveyances' open all round with only a cover on top—poor protection from wind and rain.

The Lamonds moved to Dundee in 1864. David told of some of his experiences to the reporter.

A wagon at Hatton was being loaded with potatoes, held stationary with blocks of stone on the rails. It broke loose and started off downhill towards Newtyle station, shot through the station, and crashed into a wagon loaded with barrels of tar. Both wagons were smashed to pieces; barrels of tar were rolling all over the place, bursting, and spilling out the contents. No one was injured.

Another incident occurred after the line had been altered and the branch opened to Blairgowrie. 'It was a dark and stormy night, and the rain was falling in torrents. A cutting on the line had been made through a sand bed, and the heavy rain saturating the soft sand, had got under the rails, and lifted them up on one side, and embedded the other rail in a sandbank.

Mr Lamond was driving the last train from Blairgowrie, and had passed Newtyle, when the engine stuck in the cutting. The engine was tilted to one side at an alarming angle. To ascertain the cause of the stoppage, David jumped over the lower side of the locomotive, and plumped up to the neck in sand and water. To proceed was impossible so he backed the engine out of the quicksand and backed down to Newtyle. The officials at Newtyle were in a dilemma. A train with passengers was on its way from Dundee, and Mr Lamond's passengers were anxious to reach Dundee. After much deliberation it was arranged that Mr Lamond would take his train up to the block, and there stop the train from Dundee and exchange passengers. By that arrangement Mr Lamond would return to Blairgowrie and the other train go back to Dundee.

'Mr Lamond reluctantly consented to the arrangement. Driving slowly up the incline, and keeping a keen look-out, he suddenly caught sight of the lights of the approaching train rounding a curve about four hundred yards off, and coming on at full speed. It was only a single line and a smash was imminent. Promptly he shut off steam, turned on backwards, and, when within a very short distance, he got under weigh downhill. His train dashed into the station, and got on to the loop line, just as the other train drew up at the platform. It was a narrow escape, but he saved both trains and the sacrifice of many lives. It turned out that the surfacemen had received notice of the damage, and had repaired it.'

Since he first entered the service, one of the best improvements to the line was protection for the driver and fireman. They used to have to stand on the footplate in all weathers—rain, hail, snow, sleet and wind.

Mr and Mrs Lamond had five sons and daughters and 23 grandchildren all living in Dundee. One of the sons, D. G. Lamond, held a responsible position in Strathtay House, High Street, Dundee, belonging to Mr Adam Smail. Another son was W. B. Lamond, the artist.

Canals

Thoughts about building a canal through Strathmore dates back to about 1760. The idea was to transport bulky material, such as coal, lime, farm produce, linen, etc., between Perth and the coast at Stonehaven, Montrose or Arbroath. In 1767 William Keir surveyed the Strath from Perth. In 1770 Watt proposed a 30-mile lockless canal from Kinnoull Hill, Perth, through Coupar Angus to Forfar, but no action was taken. In 1788 George Dempster of Dunnichen employed Robert Whitworth to survey for a canal from Arbroath to within two miles of Forfar at a cost of £17,788. Most of the opposition to these schemes came from those who feared that the water supply to the mills would be diverted.

In 1817 the magistrates of Arbroath commissioned Robert Stevenson to re-survey the route from Arbroath to Forfar, but the cost, £88,378, was too much.

A further report was made six years later but the whole scheme was finally abandoned in 1825. If it had been carried out, Arbroath could have been a larger town. Anyway the Dundee to Newtyle Railway was built as a means of access to Strathmore.

By 1800 the Strathmore peat was fairly exhausted and more coal was needed. The Strath had no coal. The cheapest method of transporting bulky agricultural products, lime and coal, was either by wagon or by barge. The engineering difficulties in both cases would put costs up to such an extent that a canal was unthinkable, and cost was, eventually, too much for rail.

Roads

Before 1800 turnpike roads linked Dundee with Strathmore. The road past Newtyle would follow the old bridle path fairly closely. It started at the village of Lochee and wound up the 'Birkie Brae.' Where the Kingsway-Coupar Angus roads meet at the roundabout, a road known as the 'Mile Road' or 'Milie' met the turnpike road from Clepington Road.

There was a toll-house at Auchterhouse (or Dronley) and another one half-way along the straight stretch just north of Newtyle towards Meigle—on the east side of the road. The tolls collected there paid for the upkeep of the road. But due to the tolls and the delays, the carriage of goods was expensive and slow—another reason for thinking about canals and railways.

An 'omnibus' ran between Glamis station and Kirriemuir and Forfar—horse-drawn of course. It was not until the early 20th century that horses were replaced by oil, then the roads became busier and still unsuitable for this traffic—dusty in dry weather and muddy in wet. (Sometime between 1910 and 1915 a horse-bus ran between Reid's stables at Stobswell, Dundee, and Forfar).

To cut down speed on roads, limits were imposed through towns and villages. We find Wm. J. Adam from Alyth driving through Newtyle in a single-cylinder 8 h.p. Rover at 16 m.p.h. when the speed limit was 10 m.p.h.—fined two guineas. (*Courier*, 18 April 1972).

Chapter 7

LEISURE

Newtyle Musical Society

This society was started by Thomas Honeyman in September 1880. Between 1882 and 1883 it was run by Alex Forbes. They used the school for instrument practice on Saturday mornings, and held an annual concert, also in the school [78].

There is a gap in the records from 1883 to 1903, when the funds of the society (9/-) were donated to Newtyle Public Library [76].

'Dancie' Reid [127].

John Reid was born at Auchteralyth in 1869, attended Ruthven school and became a ploughman. His first dancing teacher was James Neill, the Forfar dancer who taught Lady Elizabeth Bowes-Lyon; later consort of King George VI), and her brother David. 'Dancie' Neill must have seen unusual talents in John Reid, because Neill gave him extra coaching, and encouraged John to enter competitions at Highland games. In his second attempt he won at Airlie Games. John never forgot a piece of advice Neill gave him—'Remember—a'e glass o' whiskey does a man guid; two does him nae hairm; but three's no enough!'

At 18 John launched out on his own as a dancing teacher and enrolled 72 pupils at his first dancing class in Alyth. The fact that he knew no music hindered his ambitions, and, it was unheard of, in these days, that a dancing master could not play an instrument. So he learned to fiddle under William Jack of Ewnie, Glamis (who incidentally made violins as well as play them). Reid would walk from Airlie to Ewnie once a week for his lesson—a distance of about 5 miles. He learned bowing for strathspeys from James Hill of Alyth; and for reels from John Moncur of Nevay. At the Edinburgh Mod of 1898 he was good enough to win a gold medal.

John Reid came to Newtyle in 1894 renting a house in Belmont Street till 1911; then renting 'Craigmyle,' Commercial Street and buying it three years later. He had two sons and two daughters. His family was his orchestra—augmented on special occasions. John played the violin; his wife, Isabella, the double bass; his son, John, the piano; James played the clarionet; and Bessie, the flute and piccolo. His youngest daughter did play the violin but she was too young to play in the band.

The orchestra played all over at dances and festivals—notably at the International Folk Dancing in the Albert Hall, London, and at the Scottish Country Dance Society's summer school at St Andrews.

John also composed music and has commemorated the work of the Scottish Country Dance Society by composing 'The Scottish Country Dance Society Meeting at St Andrews'; 'The Lord James Stewart Murray's Strathspey' in honour of the president; 'Mrs Stewart of Fasnaclioch's Reel'

82

in honour of the honorary secretary and founder of the society; and 'Miss Jean Milligan's Favourite' in recognition of her untiring service to the movement. He made records published by Edison Bell and Great Scot (Megginch Castle) and broadcast on B.B.C. radio. He taught in Newtyle School and various other country schools; and in halls at Meigle, Alyth, Coupar Angus, and Blairgowrie; and in the Convent of the Sacred Heart at Bridge of Earn. Before buses or car, he would cycle with his fiddle on his back, and often walked, carrying meals or getting a meal somewhere. His children's classes were between 4 and 6 p.m. and adults from 8 to 10 p.m. at 7/6 for 12 lessons, which included the 'ball' on the last night. Eventually he did have a car.

John Reid taught in the old way—playing while he taught or demonstrated. He was strict, especially in the etiquette of the dance floor. Girls and boys were ranged separately down each side of the hall, in order of height, and partnered off—whether one liked one's partner or not. Then John would call out 'Now! gentlemen' (12 years and under!). The boy had to march across the hall, bow and offer his arm to the girl. After each dance he had to escort the girl back to her seat, on his arm, and bow before leaving her. Later in the evening the teenagers and adults also had to obey every rule. The men had to wear patent leather shoes, and, for the ball at the end of the course, they also had to wear white gloves.

'Dancie' taught four reels—the Scotch (foursome); the Reel of Tulloch; the Eightsome Reel; and the Sixteensome Reel. The dances in his repertoire included all those taught by 'Dancie' Neill, and in addition, the Blue Bonnets, Meg Merrilees, Scottish Reform, the Rock and the Wee Pickle Tow, Torryburn Lasses, and My Love She's But a Lassie Yet. He also taught the Quadrilles, the Lancers, La Russe, Circassian Circle, Waltz Country Dance, Dashing White Sergeant, Ninepins, and many circle dances. In his general classes he taught various step dances without extra charge.

As already mentioned, he taught the normal etiquette of the ballroom. But he also taught 'callisthenics,' and woe betide any misbehaviour—that got a rap on the head with the fiddle-bow.

He was a judge of highland dancing all over Scotland, usually in company with David Grewar of Mill of Camno, Meigle. Twice these two judged at the Braemar Gathering, and, by special invitation, he took a team of boy and girl dancers, drawn from his pupils in Angus and Perthshire, to give an exhibition. This was the first time girls had danced at Braemar.

On Friday afternoon, 23 October 1942, John Reid was conducting the finishing assembly of a dancing class in the Ogilvie Arms Hotel, Kirriemuir, when he collapsed. He was taken to Meigle Cottage Hospital, where he passed away at 7 o'clock the next morning, aged 73.

Sources—*Kirriemuir Free Press*, 29 October 1942;
People's Journal, 7 November 1942;
Evening Telegraph, 23 February 1960;
People's Journal, 9 August 1969;
Dundee Courier, 26 November 1969;
also John's son, the late James Reid, 52 George Street, Coupar Angus.

Newtyle Literary Society

The first record of this society was in 1878 with James Knox as President. They met in the school [78].

By 1880 the Rev. George Bell Lunan was President and a Mr Wood as secretary. Mr Lunan gave the opening address on 27 October on 'Lessons in Literature.' He even had his address printed by William Burns, 102 Nethergate, Dundee [53].

In 1881 they held an annual festival in the school, but by this time John Jack was the leading light. He wrote a play, and acted as stage manager. With a local painter he made a back-drop depicting Bannatyne House [73]. Before the end of 1881 the Society was defunct. They donated their books to the Newtyle Public Library [76].

There was a tentative revival in October 1931, with the title 'Newtyle Literary and Debating Society.' They used the school for one night per week at a rent of 2/6. John R. Pollock was secretary. He went abroad in 1934 and the Society flopped [79].

Drama

The Newtyle Dramatic Society started in 1894 when they put on the play 'Rob Roy' in the Wharncliffe Hall on Friday 16 February. They practised in the school on three evenings per week [78]. Robert Henry played Captain Thornton and Ernest Sim (estate office clerk) played Dougal Critter. John Jack made the scenery and Robert Henry painted it. Amateur photographer, Robert Henry, took photographs, developed and printed them. One of these is in the Newtyle Local Collection.

This may have been the only production of the Society as no other records have been found. In February 1937 the Newtyle Amateur Dramatic Society produced one of Joe Corrie's Scots comedies 'Tulleycairn' in the Wharncliffe Hall. Practices were held in the school. Charles Ballantine was producer and William K. Hall, local grocer, was secretary as well as acting in the play.

Again there is a gap in the information available. The Society must have been in abeyance during the war, and re-started about 1948 with the headmaster, William W. Colvin, as one of the instigators. They certainly produced plays from 1956 to at least 1965.

The Society took part in the Scottish Community Drama Association's area competitions. In 1956 they were runners-up for the Hunter trophy with the play 'Hangman's Noose' by T. M. Watson. Then in 1960 they won the trophy with David A. Adamson's play 'I walked from Philiphaugh,' produced by Miss Mary Honey.

Since about 1965 the Society became defunct probably because of lack of support, and especially lack of players.

Village Hall

There was no village hall before 1884. Any function was held in the school or in the church hall(s).

The Wharncliffe Hall was built in 1835 as a United Presbyterian (Seceeder) Church, and in 1884 it was gifted to the village under trusteeship and named after the Earl of Wharncliffe. The trustees from 1884 to 1916 included Andrew Whitton of Couston, who was factor to the Wharncliffe estate. From 1917 to 1953 various people acted as trustees, but there was no indication of the method of appointing them.

Then the Village Committee took over the trusteeship, and later in 1961 the Monifieth District Council took over the hall but left the day-to-day running to the Village Committee.

The old Free Church in Belmont Street was used as a church hall from 1900 until it was bought by the local branch of the British Legion in 1951. The new Free Church built in 1900 became the parish church hall when the churches united in 1938.

Newtyle village has often been spoken of as over-halled with three halls—Wharncliffe, Church and Legion—for a population of under 1,000. All three are old churches and none are really suitable for modern usage.

Youth Clubs

A number of efforts have been made to start youth clubs in the village since 1950. Previous to that there were Temperance Societies and Bands of Hope, but no real effort was made to give facilities to the youth.

The church did its best in the 1950s and we do find some isolated successes. For example the local church youth club put on the play 'The story of Ruth' by L. de Garde Peach, at the Festival of Community Drama in the Town Hall, Blairgowrie, on 24 and 25 February 1964. It was entered as a guest team, non-competitive. The producer was the minister, Rev. John Sherrard, with Jack Guthrie, local grocer, as stage-manager.

By 1962 the Angus Education Authority set up the Sidlaw Youth panel, covering Auchterhouse, Birkhill and Muirhead, Kettins, Lundie, Newtyle, Strathmartine, and Tealing. The committee was composed of two ministers, three headmasters and two others. For four years they held a road race from Camperdown gates to Newtyle. Various clubs, including Sea Scouts, entered individuals and teams. In June 1968 and 1969 the Sidlaw Youth Panel were holding Gala Sports Days in the various parks—Newtyle (1968) and Birkhill (1969).

Then an area youth organiser was appointed by the Education Committee in the 1970s. He was based at Muirhead and had the assistance of paid part-time youth workers.

Uniformed Organisations

The Boy Scouts were in existence in 1941 with R. B. Sinclair, banker, in charge. He was later helped by David Hain and someone from the castle called Rudi. They carried on for a year or two then packed up. The Scouts re-started in 1952 with Robert Shepherd as Scoutmaster. He became District Commissioner in 1968.

The Girl Guides were started on 22 August 1934 with an inaugural meeting held in the school. Lady Cayzer was in the chair. The first meeting of the Guides took place in the school on 1 September, with Miss Ella Joiner as Captain and Miss Turnbull as Lieutenant. The Guides also met on Saturday afternoons in the school for 2-hour cookery lessons.

To raise funds they held various functions each year—basket whists, cake and candy sales, etc. They got off to a good start with 27 guides in the company. In December 1939, despite the war, it was decided to start Brownies.

The Captain, Miss Joiner, resigned in 1943 and her place was taken by Mrs Mazurkiewicz (known as Mrs Findlay). By 1944 there were 33 guides and 27 brownies. Less than two years later Mrs Findlay resigned, and Miss McLean of Keillor became Captain. By 1946 there was a lapse in the activities.

The Newtyle Guide Company was reformed in February 1953 with Lady Cayzer as President; Mrs R. Shepherd as Captain; Mrs Laidlaw and Miss Joiner as Lieutenants. Brown Owl was Mrs Storrie and Tawny Owl was Miss Nancy Fenwick.

In 1954 Lady Cayzer gave them a hall—what was locally known as the 'Jam Factory.' It was for the exclusive use of Guides, Scouts, and Red Cross organisations at a nominal rent of £1 per year. A lot was done to the 'hut'— electric light, plumbing and heating, linoleum, outside stair renovated, and a fire escape built.

Lady Wedderspoon retired from Divisional and District Commissioner in 1965 after 10 years in office. Mrs Jamieson, Dalnaglack, South Street, took her place.

British Legion

The Newtyle and District branch of the British Legion (Scotland) was formed in 1937. The branch was in three sections—Newtyle; Auchterhouse; Muirhead/Birkhill.

The officials were—

President	Brigadier W. R. MacDonald
Hon. President	Sir Charles W. Cayzer
Chairman	Alfred Anderson
Vice-Chairman	F. K. Smith (Auchterhouse)
Secretary & Treasurer	W. K. Hall.

The membership in 1937 was 37. It rose to 75 in 1938 and to 110 in 1945. Since then the decline was slow but sure until by 1956 it reached 37. Then it fell to a handful in the 1970s, and the branch gave up.

In 1951 they purchased the old Free Church hall for £71. The slates were sold for £58. Then by 1958 the renovations had been completed at a cost of £890 including the furniture. The Newtyle branch of the W.R.I. donated £200 towards this cost. Practically all the labour was voluntary.

John Watt was hall caretaker from 1951 till nearly his death in 1973, and at a very nominal salary.

The leading light for many years was Hugh Hunter, who held most of the offices at various times. When he died in 1976 the local Legion was finished.

V.A.D. and Red Cross

The Voluntary Aid Detachment was started some years ago, and, although not apparently active, is now concerned mainly with meals-on-wheels.

The British Red Cross Society existed in 1943 when Miss Ella Joiner used the school for cookery classes. About 1950 there was a unit of the junior cadets numbering about 20, under Miss Morna MacDonald and Miss Maggie Bell.

The Rural

Two years after the Scottish Women's Rural Institute started, the Newtyle branch was formed at a meeting in the U.F. Church hall (Legion hall) on 31 October 1919. A committee was formed with Mrs Arnton, Dunarn House, as president; Mrs Sturrock, Belmont Street, as vice-president; Mrs Bell, Balgownie, as secretary; and Mrs Sim, Mundamalla, as treasurer.

The first meeting was held on Thursday 13 November at 7 p.m. By 1921 they were holding a children's treat at or near Christmas, the first one with a cinematograph show. This treat has continued up to the present day.

The 'Rural' exhibited in the Newtyle Horticultural Society's show from 1921 to the present day (with an interval for the war). Most of their exhibits were in the industrial and baking section, which occupied about half the show. Perhaps it was not the more colourful half until flower arrangement became more popular in the 1960s. They also ran their own bulb competition in spring, and entered the Horticultural Society's bulb show from 1921 to 1939.

The various branches would visit each other. The visitors put on the show, which may have been anything from the can-can to brush-making.

Each year some kind of picnic or trip was organised, e.g. a trip to the Pass of Killiecrankie in June 1922; a picnic amongst the beeches behind Kinpurnie Castle in June 1923; trips to St Andrews in 1924, to Arbroath in 1926, to Dunfermline in 1927, and to Carnoustie in 1928. The numbers taking part in these outings gradually dropped till 1931 when the trips were stopped.

They issued a syllabus (120 were printed in 1923) of the programme of their meetings. These meetings varied. Between 1920 and 1930 there were talks on raffia-work and tray-making; the 'Great Knuts' concert party; instruction in dramatic acting and folk-dancing; Burns nights; cooking; demonstrations of passe-partout; Hallowe-en parties; magic lantern entertainments; class in paper mache; making salads, meat roll and mutton pies; talk on house-keeping; demonstration and samples from Heinz; sealing-wax craft; talk on the romance of the needle; demonstration of soft toy making; demonstration from Brown and Poulson.

To collect money for running costs and various activities the Rural ran whist drives; dances; subscriptions; sales; concerts, etc. They even had a collection box in the post office from 1921 to 1923.

At the start of their life the Rural met in the U.F. Church hall, but by June 1923 the meeting place was in Mundamalla garage. The committee met there in summer and in the library in winter. The local British Legion bought the old U.F. Church hall in 1951. From then to 1977 this was their meeting place.

The members used to set out to 'let their hair down' and enjoy themselves. Much of the entertainment, especially on visits to other Rurals, would include 'dressing-up.' They even had a 'jazz band' in 1922 (the music did not matter). The Angus Federation presented 'A pageant of Angus history' at Panmure House, Carnoustie, in 1930. Newtyle took part.

One of the leading lights in the Rural for many years was Miss Nettie Briggs, daughter of William Briggs, butcher, North Street. She was on the first committee elected in 1920. Her first effort in 1923 was training a choir of members to compete in the Dundee Musical Festival. From then onwards until at least 1930, she produced plays and operettas every year. Examples of these were—'Barrin' o' the door' (1925); 'Raja of Rajapore' (1929), and 'Legend of St Yvonne' (1930).

Miss Nettie, as she was known, became president from 1939 to 1952, and Honorary President from 1957 until her death in February 1965.

The Flower Show

The Newtyle and District Horticultural Society was started about 1913. It stopped about 1939 and re-started in 1952. They held a show in August each year of flowers, fruit and vegetables, with the Rural and individuals doing the industrial and baking work. They also held a bulb show in spring from 1921 to 1939.

These dates are only estimates, because the early minutes of the Society have been destroyed, leaving a lot of scrappy information and hearsay. One of these hearsays, which may be true, is that the first show in 1919 was opened by Elizabeth Bowes-Lyon (consort of King George VI).

The secretary was William Simpson from 1952 until his death in 1966.

CHEMICAL WORKS 1886

Left to right:
1. — ;   3. — ;   5. D. Ballantine;   7. J. Webster;   9. —;
        2. C. Ballantine;   4. — ;   6. P. McOwen;   8. W. Davidson;   10. W. Smith

Manufactured bone meal: linseed oil: and oil-cake.

THE SMIDDY

Stewart McFarlane   William Fenwick   James Fenwick
                               c.1920

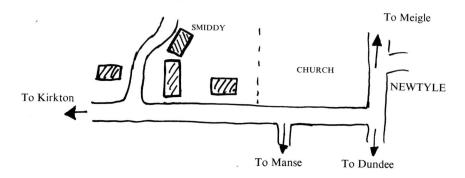

See also 41, 43, 44, 175, 265, 315

Chapter 8

THE GAMES THEY PLAYED

Bowling

The Newtyle Bowling Club was started in 1910 with 44 members at a subscription of 7/6. There was also financial assistance from patrons such as Lady Cayzer; Thomas Wedderspoon of Castleton, Eassie; Professor M'Intosh of Nevay Park; Andrew Whitton of Couston; and Herbert Ogilvie of Auchterhouse. The Club paid the Park Trustees 7/6 per member, leaving themselves with what they could raise by other means. They held a bazaar in Dundee (probably Kinnaird Hall, Bank Street) in 1910 to raise funds.

The first membership card states the bye-laws briefly and concisely:

1. No dogs to be admitted within the gates to the green.
2. No bowl to be thrown on the green.
3. No person to be allowed to play with tacketed boots or shoes.
4. Spitting on the green or in the ditch strictly prohibited.

It seems that at this time no overshoes were worn.

The fact that all the membership fees were handed over to the Park Trustees meant that the Trustees looked after the green, employing a park-keeper. The first session started late—21 May—and the green was in very poor condition. Despite this the Club played 3 away and 5 home matches. By 1911, with a very dry summer, Newtyle green had the reputation of being the worst in the district—but they played 10 matches.

Some work was done in 1912 to improve the green, but it did not open until 1 June. By the second half of the summer it had improved—having been close-cropped by scythe, and the Park Trustees had provided overshoes.

For the first time the Club was allowed by the trustees to have a direct share in the management of the green. They first dressed the green with fertiliser, etc., at a cost of £4 10s 0d.

The war years were a difficult time. In 1915 there were 44 members, falling to 30 in 1916-7, and 26 in 1918. Ladies' bowling was started in 1916. All matches were dropped, but they did run competitions, collecting £2 11s 6d in 1915 and £4 3s 0d in 1916 for the Belgian Relief Fund. In 1916 ladies were admitted to the Club at a subscription of 5/-, but at the A.G.M. there were not sufficient members to form a committee.

In 1920 the Club met with the Park Trustees to reconsider a working basis, financial and otherwise. The arrangement was a bit complicated—the Club were to pay £37 10s 0d a year plus 10/- for the use of twelve pair of bowls for the season, and they were to keep all the visitors' fees, The park-keeper was to look after the Club's interests, and be reimbursed by the Club in whatever way the members thought fit. Mr McRae, Dundee Parks Superintendent, costed the green renovation at £40. In 1922 the Club' got the sole management of the green.

Subscriptions were now 12/6 and 6/- for ladies and minors under 18. They also bought three seats, some pairs of overshoes, and held a sale of work in the park. Their share of the park-keeper's wages came to £30. In 1923 they were providing teas in the pavilion at 1/- per head. Up to now the grass was cut with a scythe, but in 1926 the Club bought its first lawn-mower.

One incident worth mentioning, was in 1932 when Canmore (Forfar) Club refused to play a match, because they considered that Newtyle was not a private club. Newtyle appealed to the Forfarshire Cup Committee, who upheld the appeal and deemed Newtyle to have won. Newtyle got a bye to play Forfar in the third round.

By the second world war only 8 to 12 players turned up at the annual meeting. It was difficult to get a green-keeper, and the Club reached the stage when they offered £5 as yearly rent to the Park Trustees instead of £20. Things improved after the war.

By 1950 Sunday bowling from 2 to 9 p.m. was started despite opposition from some organisations in the village. Subscriptions were £1 per year and visitors 6d per game. The rent was £70. Subs went up to £1 5s 0d in 1953; to £1 10s 0d in 1957; to £1 15s 0d in 1961; and to £2 in 1964.

In April 1954 the pavilion was wired for electricity, replacing the paraffin lamp.

Cricket

There seems to have been a cricket club in Newtyle from about 1908 to 1910. In 1908 they were charged 5/- towards the upkeep of the park, and by 1910 the Park Trustees were to level and sow a piece of ground for them.

The club was re-started about 1930. They ran a whist drive in the hall in February 1930, but although they had some equipment and *did* play some matches (one against Invergowrie) the club never seemed to really get going. Mostly local lads played, with the occasional few from Meigle to make up a team.

The difficulty was maintaining the pitch. This was certainly true in 1908-10, and probably in the 1930s as well. The pitch was in the middle of the park, and in the middle of a football pitch. It would need to be well and truly repaired in the spring, after being hacked about all winter.

Curling

'Newtyle (curling stone). One old specimen is still preserved—a natural quartz boulder of unshapely build, with an iron handle inserted, and weighing about 70 lbs. Smaller boulders with three finger-holes were once on the pond, entitled the 'Goose' and the 'Gander,' but they have both flown away. Other older stones were known as the 'Prince' and the 'Kebbuck'.' [46].

A far cry from the modern stone and like the Goose and the Gander, they have all flown away, without trace.

Meigle had a curling club in 1814, but there were too few inhabitants in Newtyle at that time to support a club. Although the new village of Newtyle was laid out in 1832, it was not until 1849 that a club was formed. Founder members were:

> David Hill (President) of Bannatyne House, and proprietor of the Bone Mill and the Gas Works.
> David Strathearn, Senr., mine host of the Commercial Inn.
> Charles Simpson, farmer, Hatton.
> Dr. James Mitchell, Kirkton.
> Richard Duncan, bootmaker, Kirkton.
> Thomas Lawrence, grocer and baker, Newtyle.
> Thomas Scott, retired farmer.
> Dr. Robert Langlands, Newtyle.
> George Moon, owner of the weaving factory.
> James Wilson, teacher.
> Charles Ogilvie, Nether Mill.

They met in the Commercial Inn with 15 members in 1851, charging an entrance fee of 10/6 and a yearly subscription of 2/-. This was high when one realises that a farm labourer's wages were about 2/6 per week.

In 1851 they played against Coupar Angus and Kettins for the District Medal given by the Royal Caledonian Club. Their pond was on the Glamis road just past the old level crossing. Of course, ice depended on the weather, so some years had no play—no ice! In 1852 the club considered converting the pond into a bowling green in summer, but this was not feasible.

The Annual General Meeting took place in December or January in the Commercial Inn. After the meeting came supper, then 'The court was fenced' and 'a happy evening was spent,' with the president or vice-president acting as 'croupier.' This seems to have been a stag party with an almost freemason method of initiating new members. This went by the board in 1858 when they invited ladies to the supper.

In 1855 it was found that so few turned up at the annual supper, that mine hostess, Mrs Strathearn, had a financial loss. So it was decided that those who did not turn up, would be fined 1/-!!

Membership dropped from 17 to 9 in 1854, so the entrance fee was lowered from 10/6 to 5/-, but keeping the annual subscription at 2/-. Up to the 1890s there were between 14 and 22 members, rising to 26 in the late 1890s and early 1900s, with an all-time high of 35 in 1894.

By 1856 it was decided that 'none be admitted members of this club but at the Annual General Meeting, and that by ballot (one black ball to be a refusal of the party voted for).' One interesting phrase crops up in 1865 when a 'matter was taken up between Mr Davidson and Mr Cardean to come off first ice, the loser to pay *beef and greens* . . .' This seems to mean that the loser pay for beef and vegetables for the poor, and probably in practice, meant that he gave a reasonable contribution to the local poor box.

The club usually appointed someone to be in charge of the pond as well as any hut and equipment owned by the club. The pond had to be kept clean, and someone had to get rid of the weeds, etc. In 1871 a man was employed to do this at a fixed salary of—£1 per year! By 1878 it cost £5 12s 0d to drain

91

the round pond. In 1885 water supply became difficult and a 3-inch pipe was laid from the burn at the Bone Mill entrance to the pond. There they formed a pavement cistern with overflow. The whole job cost £2 9s 0d for a distance of 80 to 100 yards.

By 1889 there was a suggestion that the club acquire a new pond. But they went ahead with an extension to the clubhouse to provide accommodation for the stones, and to pipe water from the new village supply. They also bought lamps so that they could play at night.

But it was not until 1899 that the Wharncliffe Trustees formed a new pond from the old mill pond in South Street for £60, and the club started to use it. When Sir Charles Cayzer bought the estate in 1907 he helped with the pond, and built a clubhouse charging £4 per year rent.

By 1929 the Park Trustees acted as custodian of the Curling Club funds until such time as it was re-started.

Golf

The following is taken from the minutes of the Kinpurnie Golf Club, 18 April 1912 to 9 April 1914 (the last entry).

On 18 April 1912 a public meeting was held in the Commercial Hotel with Dr. Johnstone as chairman, to inaugurate a golf club. Some initial work had already been done, as Mr Thoms, architect, was able to read out the conditions laid down by Sir Charles Cayzer for a lease of the ground. These included: 1. A 5-year lease at annual rent of £25.

2. Sir Charles to reserve the right of grazing.

There is no indication of the number present at this meeting. The office-bearers appointed were:

Captain	W. T. Ramsay.
Vice-Captain	A. Hutcheson.
Hon. Secretary	Albert Lamond.
Hon. Treasurer	Fred Will.
Committee	R. J. H. Johnstone.
	Dr. Hugh Johnston.
	Alex Millar.
	F. H. Thoms.
	David Wighton.

The annual subscription was fixed at 20/- for gentlemen and 10/- for ladies. Sir Charles Cayzer became Honorary President and Edward Cox of Cardean became Hon. Vice-President.

The post of greenkeeper was advertised at £40 per year plus 10% of the visitors' fees. He was to work 32 hours per week on the course during the summer and 16 hours in winter. He also had to be able to coach and mend clubs. Rules were made up but there is no copy in the minutes.

By 13 June they were finding that the six holes in Bannatyne Park were in very poor condition. A road was to be started but there is no further mention of it.

The committee took exception to the 6th clause of the lease with Sir Charles. This read: 'The second parties (the golf club) shall accept responsibility for any accident to stock, which may happen in consequence of ground being used as a Golf Course.' The club proposed that this clause be either deleted or modified, and that they refuse the lease as it stands. There is no indication of the outcome of this motion.

On 5 July 1912 W. T. Ramsay resigned both as Captain and as member of the club. This was not explained in the minutes, but it does indicate some argument or disagreement. On 6 August 1912 W. R. Macdonald was appointed Captain.

Sir Charles agreed to open the course officially some time after 10 September 1912. But this was postponed.

The greenkeeper was asked to cut the thistles on the course in his spare time at 6½d per hour. Lost balls were a trouble (they always are) and the club's solution was that the greenkeeper re-sell them at 3d each—1d to the finder (usually the farmer, Mr Sime); 1d to the greenkeeper and 1d to the club. Mr Simpson (professional at Carnoustie) and Mr Kirkcaldy were engaged to play over the course at the opening, at a fee of three guineas plus expenses. But the Captain took Mr Simpson over the course at his own expense. Mr Simpson stated that 'he would not care to ask a brother professional to play over the course in its condition.' A lot of work was needed, estimated at £150 so the opening was postponed. Sir Charles offered a loan of £100 at 5% and the club decided to hold a bazaar in conjunction with the Curling Club in November 1912.

In April the club was asked to vacate three holes on Auchtertyre Hill, for which they would get the field on Auchtertyre farm west of the course.

Costs may be of interest. The club's estimates for renovating the course in October 1913 were:

Six greens (teeing)	£15
Two putting greens	£60

The club had some kind of hut, because in May 1913 they had 17 club boxes erected by Mr McKenzie, the local joiner, at a cost of 3/6 each. These were to be rented out at 3/6 per year. Later in 1914 this was reduced to 1/6.

Three people—A. Easson, George McLaren, and Gibson Smith—were admitted as artisan members. There is no indication of the fees they paid.

At last the course was opened in August 1913 and Kirkcaldy did play over it. Luncheon cost 4/- and the hire of the marquee £2 2s 0d. In November 1913 the club was in financial difficulties. Sir Charles was approached but he stated 'that he considered he had fulfilled all his obligations to the club.' The club called in a Mr Hunter of Glasgow (presumably an expert) to inspect the course and report on it.

Another indication of trouble was the resignation of W. R. Macdonald from the captaincy which he had held since August 1912. The committee refused to accept his resignation until he attended a committee meeting and explained 'certain matters in connection with the opening of the course.'

By January 1914 the club was raising a loan among themselves. Despite the apparent hardening attitude of Sir Charles towards the club, and the continual approach to him for help, he still accepted the position of Honorary

President at the A.G.M. in the U.F. Church hall on 2 April 1914. John A. Cox, J. F. Fyffe-Jamieson and Thomas Wedderspoon were Hon. Vice-Presidents. James Reid was made Captain, A. C. Hutcheson had been Vice-Captain from the start, and the banker, F. Will, had been Treasurer. And—for the first time a lady secretary was appointed—Miss Beaton.

The last entry in the book is 9 April 1914, when they raised the green-keeper's salary to £1 per week.

Putting

In September 1923 the Park Trustees decided to lay out a 'golf putting green' at a cost not to exceed £10. By March 1924 they allowed an extra £3. The green was completed by May that year. Charges were to be 5/- per season or 1d per round. Balls and putters were supplied at the pavilion.

The park-keeper, Andrew Donaldson, took on the green in addition to his normal duties at an extra 15/- per week for the season. W. R. Macdonald offered a silver cup for competition on the putting green.

It seemed to go quite well, because by September 1924 the green was extended to 18 holes, and the park-keeper was given £4 as a bonus. The trustees also purchased a motor mower in 1925 at a cost of £20.

Costs must have risen by 1927 because the putting fees were put up to 2d per round or 7/6 per year, with children at 1d per round—for 16 holes.

An attempt was made to run the putting green as a club, but this failed.

By May 1940 the putting green was given up—it had not paid its way for quite a number of years. And there was a war on.

Quoits

Quoits is a very old game—said to have been started by King James IV—but it became popular from 1880 to 1914, dwindling gradually from 1918 to the 1930s, surviving especially in the mining areas. In 1970 it was revived in Wales where there were 12 clubs by 1971. There was only one club in Scotland—the Dunottar Quoiting Club of Stonehaven, which celebrated its 80th birthday in 1970.

Between 1880 and the 1930s nearly every village or district had its quoiting club, and of course that included Newtyle. This club played on spare ground on the south side of west Church Street. The photograph of the Newtyle Quoits Club in the Newtyle local collection can only be dated at a guess between 1890 and 1900. The pair of quoits also in this collection were made by Houston of Johnstone, Renfrewshire, and could have been made any year after 1900, but the likeliest date is about 1920. This pair have the 'horse-shoe' grip, and are marked as 16½ lbs. They are weighed in pairs and this pair had been bored down to 7½ lbs each, then partly loaded with lead to the original weight (or any weight in between to suit the player). In 1937 a pair of Houston quoits cost 2/6 per lb. So far, all that remains of the Newtyle Quoiting Club are the photograph and the pair of quoits. (For most of this information I am indebted to James G. Murdoch, secretary of the Dunnotar Quoiting Club 1971).

The rules of the game are briefly:

(1) The distance from hob to hob be 18 yards.

(2) Heads to be 2ft 6ins in diameter, of clay, and the pin or hob to be level with the clay.

(3) Pins or hobs to be 2ft 6ins long by $1\frac{1}{4}$ins in diameter and tapered down 7 inches to be $\frac{1}{2}$in diameter at top clay level.

(4) Quoits of any weight to suit the player but not more than $8\frac{3}{4}$ inches in diameter,

(5) The nearest edge of quoit to the nearest edge of the top of the pin or hob to count 1 point. If both player's quoits are nearer than his opponent's he scores two points.

(6) A quoit that rolls on does not count and should be thrown off by the referee.

(7) A game is 21 points.

(8) A team is of 8 players and 2 reserves, and the team captains appoint a referee before play starts. The referee's decision is final.

(9) A player cannot change his quoits in the middle of a game unless one quoit gets broken, and then only with the consent of his opponent *and* the referee, can he do so. If his opponent objects he must finish the game with one quoit.

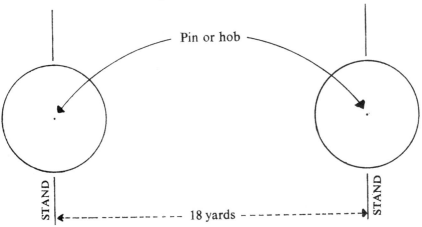

Players throw from end to end and stand with toes on line marked 'stand.' Each player has a marker who puts a piece of paper two inches before the pin, and the player throws to the paper which is his guide to where the pin is. The markers also keep the score.

Tennis

There was a tennis club about 1900 playing on courts at the north end of Commercial Street, on the other side of the old level crossing. In 1910 the public park was formed and tennis courts built. The club then existed up to the 1939-45 war.

In 1947 it was re-formed. The committee consisted of Miss Margaret Bell, secretary and treasurer; Miss Jessie Donaldson; Miss Hamilton; Messrs. S. Cathro, G. Milne, R. B. Sinclair, banker, and W. W. Colvin, headmaster. They were active for a number of years holding whist drives, socials, etc., to gather money. By 1949 they received the gift of a cup from Lady Cayzer, which was designated for the ladies' singles, and the club bought another one for the men's singles.

There was some bother with junior players who complained that they got very little playing or coaching, especially in the evenings. There was a move in 1950 to try to give them some coaching.

From 1958 the membership dropped, and with a rent of £70 per year for the three courts, running the club became difficult. They ran a big raffle each year from 1960-5, but membership was very low, and some of the original members had either gone or took no interest. On 11 April 1967 it was decided with regret to disband.

By this time the stanchions and wire netting round the courts were in a very poor condition. The cost of renovation of two courts was too much (£2,000 at the time) even for the Village Committee. The stanchions were removed before they collapsed and the courts were left in the hope that some day they could be revitalised.

The Park

On 16 October 1905 a public meeting was held in the old Free Church in Belmont Street (Legion Hall), to consider setting up a public park. Robert Sim of Mundamalla was chairman with James D. Morgan, headmaster, as clerk.

Some comments and reasons for having a park, put at that meeting, are worth noting:

Dr. Mills thought that a park was a necessity for young ones.

Rev. William Maxwell thought that a park would attract summer visitors 'and make Newtyle the more popular summer resort that it was fitted by nature to be.'

Dr. Johnston said that the park would enhance the feu value.

George Dingwall, retired gardener, was down to earth by bringing up the general complaint of the village at the time that 'we need a dumping ground for rubbish.' (Did he mean the park??)

They decided to arrange a meeting with Mr Brebner, factor to the Cayzer estate; to raise funds by voluntary effort, not by rates; to have cricket, football, tennis and bowling; to suggest, as a site, the field immediately west of the Bannatyne Avenue.

Sir Charles offered the old nursery park, about $5\frac{1}{2}$ acres, on a lease of 19 years at half the agricultural value. The committee wanted a longer lease, because 19 years was a short time if they wanted to erect a pavilion. Sir Charles stuck to his guns, but gave assurance of renewal, as long as plans for any buildings were approved by him. The lease was signed on 9 March 1907.

Money was raised by a concert in the winter and a bazaar in the summer. In the meantime Mr Sim offered a loan of £50 to start them off, and Mrs Sim presented children's swings.

96

By spring 1907 things went ahead—iron gate from Shepherd & Co., Meigle, for £16 16s 0d; two tennis courts from John Hunter, Meigle, for £21 5s 0d; water and drainage from Messrs. Gray & Sons, Newtyle, at £9 18s 0d; the drinking fountain No. 6 from Saracen Foundry, Glasgow, gifted by Mr Sim.

The concert in February 1907 raised £11 and the bazaar in the Kinnaird Hall, Dundee, netted £610, with £116 off for expenses.

By October that year the Committee decided to build a pavilion. It was finished in August 1908 at a cost of £204, and opened by Sir Charles Cayzer. The bowling green was also opened at the same time. It had a membership of 44.

The post of park-keeper was advertised. There were 126 applicants, but only 16 were suitable. Police Sergeant Whittle of Forfar was appointed at £45 per year.

The park was let out for grazing in 1910 to Mr Reid, Belmont Street, for 40 sheep, at £2 rent (increased to £4 in 1911). In 1914 it was suggested that the area between the pavilion and North Street be laid out as a croquet green, but this never came off.

In 1915 the army used the pavilion as a sergeant's mess. They were charged £1 per month. From 1917 to 1919 the park was ploughed and cropped for food—first oats then potatoes, and lastly in 1919 it was sown with corn and grass. That same year the Parish Council received a legacy of £300 from the late Dr. Mills, the interest to be used for the park.

1920 saw a change in the rent structure. Up to then only individuals were charged—bowling 15/-; tennis 15/-; or both for 25/- per year. Now clubs were being charged—for bowling £37 10s 0d per year, plus 10/- for use of bowls; for tennis £30 and for football £2. The park trustees paid £10 to re-turf and level the bowling green.

Rabbits were a bother and the trustees had to pay up to £9 for netting round the bowling green. In 1922 the tennis club got a third court, and by 1924 a putting green was started. The putting green was extended to 16 holes, but by 1940 it was given up.

Miss Simpson of Alyth presented a flagpole and had it erected in 1931. She also paid for fences, pavilion roof and walks, making a total of just over £200.

An attempt was made in 1934 to introduce Sunday tennis. But this was refused. It was 1947 before it was allowed.

To celebrate the royal jubilee in 1935 the trustees ran children's sports and fancy-dress parade. They proudly recorded that the flag was flown on the new flagpole. Miss Simpson presented new swings, planted a fir tree, and donated a railing to go round it.

Coronation year 1937 saw a donation from Miss Isabella Ogilvie of Belmont Cottage, of chute, gymnastic set, ocean wave, seats and netting.

The park was ploughed and cultivated in 1940 as a war effort. It was re-sown in 1944. In 1946 the headmaster, William Colvin, organised the school children to clean up the tennis courts on condition that the school could use them.

Chapter 9

SHOPS AND JOBS

Newtyle is too new a village to have a fair or public market. Meigle had an old traditional market in the square on Tuesdays.

The commonest seller was the travelling pack-man or 'gain'-aboot-mannie.' (*Newtyle Magazine*, September 1966). One of the local pack-men about 1880 was John Donald or John Donnart from Ardler, where he had a small shop. Mostly he went round the farm houses and cottages, but would have some sale in Newtyle village itself. His pack (two Gladstone-type carpet bags) contained such things as boot laces, blacking, tobacco, clay pipes and snuff, butter and cheese, peppermint drops, curly-wurlies for the bairns, musk lozenges, perfumed soap in fanciful shapes, matches, etc., etc. Not only did he bring goods to sell, but his arrival was looked forward to as a social occasion with the latest news.

The tinkers were another group who wandered, mending pots and pans. They made, sold and repaired baskets of all shapes and sizes from shopping and children's baskets to sculls for collecting potatoes on the field. They begged, but seldom if ever, stole. Also they were the cleanest pickers of blaeberries known.

In the Newtyle area there were the Burkes, Flynns, Whites, Stewarts, McLarens and Townsleys, among others. They returned summer after summer to the same camping ground for their legal length of stay. One of these places was an old disused lane at Kirkinch known as the 'Strip.' (*Newtyle Magazine*, August 1966).

The fishwife came from Arbroath with creels of smokies and other fish. Mrs Isa Cargill of 13 Seagate, Arbroath, came to Newtyle twice weekly for at least 47 years from 1919, first by train then by bus. Her niece, Margaret, carried on for a short time after Isa retired, but then gave it up.

Banking

James Fenton, a farmer at Eassie, was granted credit of £300 from the Dundee Banking Company between 1763 and 1767. (C. W. Boase. *A century of banking in Dundee*. 1867).

A branch of the Dundee National Security Savings Bank was opened in Newtyle in 1839. Deposits in August 1841 were £145 19s 3d and in May 1842 £139 12s 1d [101].

In 1872 a branch of the Commercial Bank of Scotland was opened at 4 Commercial Street. This was a house as well as a bank, owned by Andrew Whitton of Couston. It lasted until 1896 with the following agents—Mr Phin (1884); Mr Dickson (1884-5); James Knox (1885-6); and James Alex Webster (1886).

The Royal Bank of Scotland opened a sub-branch to Meigle on 5 June 1922. Hearsay has it that the bank functioned in the Wharncliffe Hall until it obtained premises at 24 South Street. At the start it opened from 9.30 to 12.30 on Mondays and Fridays.

Shops

The early 19th century shops would be small general shops located usually in one of the rooms of the house. At the time these houses could easily be of two rooms only. By the 1860s there were six general shops, one baker's (on the site of the present bakery and shop) and a butcher's. Ten years later there were two grocer's shops—self-styled as such although they also sold general merchandise. The total number of grocers and general merchants remained about six right up to 1918.

Specialist shops started in 1871 with a draper's shop in Belmont Street run by Mrs Gibson. This lasted until 1900. Another was opened in 1929 in North Street.

One short-lived effort in 1867-8 was a shop opened by Alex Carnegie for the sale of stoneware—jugs, jars, grey-beards, etc. Tailors did business from 1867 to 1889—William Leslie (1867-1889) and Robert Whitton (1886-1905). Both worked from their houses.

Saddlers also operated from their houses from 1881-7. By 1902 John R. Milne opened his saddler's shop in North Street but gradually changed to become an ironmongers in the 1930s.

In 1856-7 James Walker, and in 1867-8 Thomas Young, worked as shoemakers from their houses. Then Thomas Lamond had a shoemaker's shop in North Street from 1881 to the 1930s. He employed a cobbler. From about 1890 to about 1930 Andrew Cant worked as a cobbler from a room in his house in Belmont Street. When he died in September 1954 he was 93 years old.

An unusual trade for a village was a hatter. But Michael Gallacher, South Street, traded for only a year or two in 1867, then changed to keeping a lodging house. John Heron opened a watchmaker's business in Church Street between 1892 and 1897.

The post office seems to have existed from somewhere about 1880. The house Taranaki in North Street had 'Post Office' painted on the upper lintel of one of the windows in the lower flat. We do know that D. Ritchie Smith, railway clerk, also acted as postmaster from 1886 to 1889. Then John Jack's sister, Amy, kept the post office in Church Street (No. 4) from 1892 until 1910. She was followed from then to the 1930s by Elsie Gray in the same shop. From 1892 to 1910 Robert Fenwick of Church Street called himself a 'letter carrier.' Gibson Craig Smith of South Street was postman from then to the 1930s.

Refreshment rooms were opened by 1872 in North Street (No. 2) by Miss Robinson. It consisted of a bar with two other rooms, and timber-built stables and sheds. From 1911 to the 1930s Mrs Lucy Young and her family kept refreshment rooms in South Street (No. 6).

Robert Gray kept the inn in Church Street (No. 30 or 32) from 1856 to 1882, and from then to 1895 by his widow Mrs Isabella Gray. The single-storey building had a wooden turret known as 'Rabbie Gray's turret.' It had

CHURCH STREET.

From left—   John Jack's workshop c.1868 to 1899.
    No. 2 His house from 1834 to 1910.
    No. 4 Post Office from 1892 to c.1930.
    No. 6 House.

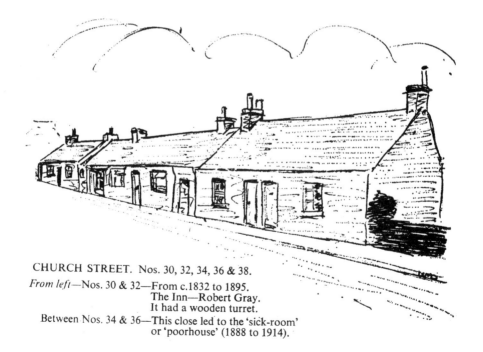

CHURCH STREET. Nos. 30, 32, 34, 36 & 38.

*From left—*Nos. 30 & 32—From c.1832 to 1895.
             The Inn—Robert Gray.
             It had a wooden turret.
Between Nos. 34 & 36—This close led to the 'sick-room'
             or 'poorhouse' (1888 to 1914).

no apparent use although hearsay had it that there was a stair up. There is some doubt about this. In 1895 the inn was used by Andrew Whitton Gray as a builder's yard.

Two hawkers lived in the village—James Millar from 1867-8 and William Duncan from 1876-7. The locations of their houses is not known.

The Commercial Inn at the corner of South Street and Commercial Street must have been built not long after the village started, and possibly by Colonel Dalgairns of Ingliston. At least he was the proprietor till 1876 with David Strathearn as tenant. Mrs Ann Strathearn bought it in 1876. The retired sea captain, David Clark Burman (who built the 'Anchorage' in Castle Street), owned the hotel from 1883 to 1885, then sold out to John Cable.

Trades

John Ireland, a mason, came from Newbigging, and built three small houses in South Street (Nos. 20 & 22), staying in one of them. The Gray family were the master masons in Newtyle from 1876 until 1940.

Two well-known slaters lived in Newtyle—John Butchart lived in 'Achterneed' (Nos. 37/39) North Street from 1881 to 1903. Maxwell Beverley lived in Belmont Street from 1898 until he retired in 1938. He worked for Crichton, builder, Meigle.

The blacksmith's shop, behind the church, was run by William Alexander about 1800 then from 1856 to 1895 by David Hardie. He was followed by John Robertson till 1908, when William Fenwick moved from the smiddy at Chapel of Keillor.

John Jack's father came to Newtyle in 1834, to live in houses he had built in Church Street. John, by 1862, had a joiner's business there, with workshops in the Dundee Road. This lasted until 1909. He employed two men and sometimes three. From 1910 to 1915 Robert McKenzie had a wheelwright's and joiner's shop behind the parish church. He employed at least one man. Andrew Anderson started up a joinery in 1915, followed by his son, Alfred, and grandson, Andrew. Andrew sold out and left the district about 1960.

Thomas Saunders operated a timber merchant's business from 1871. His sawmill was located in South Street, at the site of the old mill of Newtyle, using the mill-pond to work his machines. This lasted until about 1900. From 1888 to 1910 George Duncan worked a sawmill at Alyth Junction.

A laundry was located in North Street from 1911 to the 1950s. It was owned by John Walton and employed a few women and a van driver.

The Simpsons were the mole-catchers in Newtyle—Peter in East Church Street up to 1880, and James in the same house up to the 1930s, with a short break at East Keillor from 1898 to 1909. He was, of course, known as 'Moley Simpson.'

A rabbit-trapper, Donald Chisholm, lived at Burnside from 1896 to 1897, and another, Charles McCalley, at 22 South Street about 1930.

William Pirrie, Belmont Street, about 1876, and David Reid, also Belmont Street, from 1896 to 1907, were cattle-dealers. Robert Cowie was a horse-breaker, living at Burnside from 1876-7.

Coal merchants have been in the village since 1856. One business was owned by David Hill of Bannatyne House, who also owned the 'Bone Mill' and the gas works. Other coal merchants from 1886 to the 1930s were James Cook, George Will and John McKenzie.

At the time of the 'Volunteers,' Newtyle in line with other villages such as Glamis, had full-time drill instructors. In Newtyle there were:

1876-87 Sgt. O'Shaughnessy.
1888-9 John Jeffrey.
1890-3 Lewis J. Jago.
1894-5 James L. Duff.

As well as their jobs as drill instructors, they sometimes did odd functions such as—drilling the local school children; a bit of recruiting; and, most important, look after the armoury located usually in their house; and service their rifles, etc.

The toll house in the Meigle Road was no longer used for tolls after 1800, but the Turnpike Road Trustees were still in existence up to about 1877. The house was occupied by a tacksman, i.e. a lessee.

Probably the best recorded doctor was Dr. David Marnie Mills who lived in South Street (No. 8). He retired in 1902 and died in 1919, leaving his house to the parish church to be kept as a doctor's house. He was replaced by Dr. Hugh Johnstone who lived in North Street before occupying the South Street house in 1919. Another doctor, Alex Gillespie Smith, lived in Commercial Street from 1890 to 1905. A James Mitchell, surgeon, died at Newtyle on 6 April 1842, aged 43.

Chapter 10

SOME BRIEF BIOGRAPHIES

Maxwell Beverley

He was a native of Aberdeenshire and came to Newtyle about 1900. From then until he retired in 1938 he was employed by A. Crichton, slater, Meigle.

He served for two years in the Boer War, and was amongst Kitchener's Contemptibles in the 1914-18 war, when he was severely wounded and gained the D.C.M. He reached the rank of sergeant-major.

Between the two wars he was a member of the Territorials and for several years was drill instructor to the local detachment. For a short time before his death he was a relief Air Raid Precautions Warden.

Being very keen on football he supported Newtyle Football Club, first as player, then trainer, and thereafter as a staunch supporter.

He died suddenly on 6 February 1940.

Nettie Briggs

See under Rural, page 88.

David Clark Burman

James Burman was born at the Mill of Newtyle and Balmaw on 2 May 1777. He became the miller there. He married Cecilia Clark of Princelands (near Newtyle). She was born on 30 August 1796 and died on 11 December 1870. James died on 22 December 1839.

One of their daughters, Katherine, married Richard Baird, a civil engineer from Edinburgh, who was in charge of the Dundee/Newtyle Railway, and also the Dundee/Arbroath Railway.

James' and Cecilias' son, David Clark Burman, was born at the Mill on 7 February 1830. He became a captain in the merchant navy, and when he retired, he returned to Newtyle. He built the 'Anchorage' at the corner of Castle Street and Belmont Street, designing one of his upper rooms like the bridge of a ship.

He was a member of the Newtyle Curling Club from 1871 to 1895, holding various offices—Vice-President in 1877; Secretary/Treasurer in 1887-8; and President in 1889 and 1895.

He owned the Commercial Inn (or Hotel) from 1883 to 1885. He also purchased the old U.P. Church in 1880. This became the village hall (or Wharncliffe Hall) in 1884.

He died on 11 July 1906.

John Henry

John Henry was born at Hillton in the county of Banff in 1837. He joined the Great North of Scotland Railway Co. at the age of 20. Later he became stationmaster at Ladybridge. When the Great North and Caledonian amalgamated he acted as relief stationmaster.

He was appointed stationmaster at Newtyle in 1867, and became master of the new station in North Street. He was transferred to Dunblane, but came back to Newtyle after being persuaded by Major Thomas to become manager of the Chemical Works. He kept that position for about 40 years until the works closed down in 1911.

John died in 1923 at the age of 86. His wife pre-deceased him many years before. They had two sons, and a neice who stayed with them (Miss Kessock).

Jean Hill

Jean Young was born at Glamis in 1798. Her husband was a farm servant, who was wounded at Waterloo and died aged 45 before their youngest child was born. She rented a cottage 'with a kailyaird' on Kilmundy near Lumley Den.

She liked to sing the old Scottish ballads, and her only luxury was a smoke of her cutty pipe at the fireside. There she would reminisce of smugglers; of the year of the short corn; of the long hard winters and the snowstorms. When old she moved to live with one of her married daughters in Dundee. But she could not stand city life and removed to Newtyle.

There she spent her 100th birthday in 1898.

John Jack [30]

> 'And still the wonder grew
> That one small head could carry all he knew.'
>
> —Goldsmith.

John Jack was born in Dunkeld in 1830, where his father was a slater. His parents came to reside in Newtyle in 1834.

John learned the joinery trade in Kirriemuir and returned to Newtyle after completing his apprenticeship, and on his father's death. He spent eight years as a journeyman, then went to Dundee as architect's assistant to Mr Christopher Kerr. He returned to Newtyle about 1855, and died on 25 April 1905, aged 75.

During his time in Newtyle his interests were wide and varied. He seemed to take part in everything that went on—so much so that he earned the nickname of 'Provost.'

The following is a list of his activities and occupations, which may not be complete. The more one reads over it, the more one feels that some are missed out. Anyway here it is:

Joiner and undertaker.

Architect's assistant.

Played the bass ophlicleide, the flute, and the tenor horn, among others.

Teacher of music.

104

Free Church precenter.

Elder in the U.F. Church.

Private in the Volunteers. Retired in 1882 as Captain after 23 years service. Was band sergeant.

Lectured on bees.

A bit of a rhymer.

Wrote a play, stage directed it, made and painted the scenery—a backdrop of Bannatyne House.

Inspector of the Poor. Sanitary Inspector. Inspector of lodging houses, of dairies, etc.

Collector of rates.

Clerk to the School Board.

Secretary and treasurer to Newtyle Public Library.

Secretary to the Angus and Mearns Association of Inspectors of the Poor.

Secretary and treasurer to Newtyle Curling Club.

House-agent.

Painter and decorator.

Clock and watch repairer.

(Incidentally they were not all at the same time!!)

David Lamond

See under Railways, pp. 79-80.

Sir William Lamond

He was the son of Thomas Lamond, shoemaker, who had a shop in North Street. William was born in 1887, and educated at the Harris Academy, Dundee. In 1914 he married Ethel Minnie, daughter of Edward Speechley of Karachi. They had one son. Ethel died in 1939. His second marriage was to Norah Aitken, daughter of Edward Kiddie of St Ives, Huntingdonshire.

William joined the Royal Bank of Scotland at Meigle in 1902 and five years later went to the Bank of Bombay. He became a committee member of the Indian Central Banking in 1930-1. From 1934-45 he was managing director of the Imperial Bank of India, and during that time (1943-5) he was President of the Indian Institute of Bankers. He was knighted in 1936. He became director of the Calcutta Electric Supply Corporation from 1949 to 1969.

He died on 6 February 1974 at his home in Hurlingham, London, in his 87th year.

William Bradley Lamond

His father was David Lamond, railwayman (see pp. 79-80) who lived in Belmont Street where William was born on 23 July 1857. They came to Dundee when he was 7 years old. William worked for a time on the railway, then took up art as a career. He died of pneumonia on 3 December 1924 at his house, 25 William Street, Dundee.

As a young man attending School Wynd Church he made sketches of the Rev. George Gilfillan during his sermon. He had a small studio in Auchmithie, near Arbroath, and it was here that most of his sea-scapes and fisher-folk were painted. He exhibited in the Royal Academy and in 1902 held a one-man show at the Clifford Gallery in the Haymarket, Edinburgh. In 1903 he was elected a member of the Royal Society of British Artists.

On 16 December 1925 a memorial exhibition of 70 of his paintings was held in the Victoria Art Galleries, Dundee. It was opened by Sir Harry Lauder. This exhibition included four water-colours by W. B. Lamond.

In 1972 to celebrate the centenary of Newtyle Church, the Newtyle Village Committee set up an art exhibition, which included about 30 of W.B's oils on loan.

Professor M'Intosh [129]

William Carmichael M'Intosh was born at St Andrews on 10 October 1838, the only son of John M'Intosh, builder and town councillor of St Andrews. William was educated at Madras College and St Andrews University. He graduated M.D. with distinction and gold medal at Edinburgh University in 1860, specialising in mental disease. In 1863 he became superintendent at Perth District Asylum at Murthly.

But his main interest was always natural history. During his life he wrote a long series of papers on fauna.

In 1882 he became Professor of Natural History at St Andrews University. He occupied this chair until he retired in 1917. During this time he pioneered fishery research, and was instrumental in setting up the marine research laboratory at St Andrews. He was given many honours during his lifetime from various Royal Societies; from the Linnean Society; from the Ray Society; and from a number of universities.

He built Nevay Park near Newtyle in 1902 and commuted to St Andrews, usually by rail from Alyth Junction. He built a cairn to the south of Nevay Park and higher uphill, to celebrate the 300th anniversary of St Andrews University in 1911. He also planted a grove of specimen trees—the name plates have gone. And, according to hearsay, he collected dead rabbits with something wrong with them. For example—if the front teeth are out of alignment and miss each other, then they keep on growing piercing the other jaw, causing the rabbit's death. The animals were hung out in the open until the skeletons were clean.

Professor M'Intosh died, unmarried, on 1 April 1931. A portrait of him hangs in the rooms of the Linnean Society, Burlington House, and M'Intosh Hall in St Andrews is named after him.

His youngest sister Roberta (Mrs Gunther) was a gifted artist, and illustrated many of his works.

John Reid ('Dancie' Reid)
See under 'Leisure' pp. 82-83.

Hugh Watson (of Aberdeen/Angus cattle fame)
See under 'Agriculture' pp. 56-57.

BIBLIOGRAPHY

Numbers in brackets within the text refer to the numbers here

1. ALLEN, J. R. & ANDERSON, J. The early Christian monuments of Scotland. Edinburgh 1903.
2. ANGUS COUNTY COUNCIL. Articles on Angus. 1949-50.
3. ANGUS COUNTY COUNCIL, Education Committee. Exploring Angus. 1975.
4. ANGUS GIRL GUIDES. Angus for the disabled. Forfar 1973.
5. ANGUS HISTORIC BUILDINGS SOCIETY. Historic buildings of Angus. Forfar 1974.
6. ANTIQUARIES OF SCOTLAND, Society of. Proceedings
    v.34, 1899-1900 (Pitcur Souterrain; Denoon fort.).
    v.60, 1928 (Glass ball found at Auchtertyre).
7. op. cit. v.8, 1910 (Stone-age axe found at Hatton).
8. op. cit. v.6, 1865 (Stone found at Bannatyne House).
9. ARMSTRONG, M., and PATERSON, I. B. The Lower Old Red Sandstone of the Strathmore region. H.M.S.O., 1970 (Fossil fish at Auchtertyre farm).

10. BANNATYNE CLUB. The ancient sculptured monuments of the County of Angus. 1848 (Keillor stone).
11. op. cit. Memoir of George Bannatyne, 1545-1608. Edinburgh, 1829.
12. BARTY, J. W. Ancient deeds and other writs in the Mackenzie-Wharncliffe charter-chest. Edinburgh, 1906.
13. Bill to amend the Acts for making a Railway from Dundee to Newtyle in the County of Forfar. c1840.
14. BLACK, publisher. Picturesque tourist of Scotland. Edinburgh, 1852.
15. BLAIRGOWRIE CO-OPERATIVE SOCIETY. A short history of the co-operative movement in Blairgowrie and district. 1967.
16. BRIGGS, Messrs. William, & Sons, Ltd. The first 100 years, 1865-1965. 1967.
17. BRITISH ASSOCIATION. Handbook and guide to Dundee and district. Dundee, 1912.
18. op. cit. Dundee, 1947.
    (Souvenir presented by Messrs. Valentine & Sons Ltd.).
19. op. cit. Dundee and District, edited by S. J. Jones. Dundee, 1968.
20. BUTE manuscripts. (Collection of various fugitive material belonging to the Earl of Bute). Late 18th century.
21. BUTT, John. The industrial archaeology of Scotland, 1967 (Dundee/Newtyle Railway).

22. CAMPBELL, R. H. Scotland since 1707. 1965 (Hugh Watson).
23. CHALMERS, publisher. The gazeteer of Scotland. Dundee, 1803.
24. CRAVEN, Neil. A bibliography of the County of Angus. Forfar, 1975.
25. CRAWFORD, O. G. S. Topography of Roman Scotland. Cambridge, 1949.
26. CULROSS, printers. Strathmore illustrated. Coupar Angus, 1904.
27. CUMMING, Gershom, publisher. Forfarshire illustrated. 1848.

28. DAWSON, J. H. An abridged statistical survey of Scotland. 1857.
29. DICK, Robert. Scottish communion tokens. 1902.
30. DRYERE, Henry. Blairgowrie, Stormont and Strathmore worthies. 1903.
31. DUNDEE CORPORATION. Museums in education; a guide to the services of the City of Dundee Museums & Art Galleries. 1974.
32. DUNN, Matthias. Observations upon the line of railroad projected by Mr Landale from Dundee to the valley of Strathmore. 1825.

33. EAST CENTRAL (Scotland) REGIONAL PLANNING ADVISORY COMMITTEE. The Tay valley plan. Dundee, 1950.

34. 'Engineer,' The. v.55 March 2, 1883, pp. 156-160. Links in the history of
    Locomotive No. 14. 1833.
    (Drawings, etc. of first engine for Dundee/Newtyle Railway).
35. EWING. Annals of the Free Church of Scotland. 1914.

36. FORFARSHIRE W.R.I. Pictorial souvenir: pageant of Angus history at

    Panmure House, Carnoustie, 21 June 1930.
37. GAVINE, David. James Stewart Mackenzie (1719-1800) and the Bute MSS.
    (Journal for history of astronomy, v.1974).
38. GRANT, James. The yellow frigate. n.d. (1890?).
    (Novel containing story of cannibal of Auchtertyre).
39. GROOME, Francis H., ed. Ordnance gazeteer of Scotland. 1903.
40. GUTHRIE, James Cargill. Vale of Strathmore. 1875.

41. HEADRICK, Rev. James. General view of the agriculture of the county of
    Angus or Forfarshire. Edinburgh, 1813.

42. IMPERIAL gazeteer of Scotland. c1871.

43. JERVISE, Andrew. Memorials of Angus and Mearns. 1861.
44. JOINER, Henry. Newtyle past and present. Coupar Angus, 1962.
45. JOINER, Henry. Weather records, 1949-1965. Ms.
    (Local headmaster who kept official weather station).

46. KERR, John. History of curling. Edinburgh, 1890.
47. KERR, R. Communion tokens of the Church of Scotland. Proceedings of
    Society of Antiquities of Scotland, v.5, 7th series. 1942-3.
48. KINPURNIE GOLF CLUB. Minute book, 1912-14. Ms.

49. LAMB, J., ed. Fasti of the U.F. Church, 1900-29. 1956.
50. LITTLEJOHN, C. E. S. The Dundee and Newtyle Railway. ('The Railway
    Magazine,' 1910-11).
51. LOCKHART, D. G. The evolution of the planned villages of north-east Scotland:
    studies in settlement geography, c1700-c1900. 2 vols., 1974. Ms.
    (Thesis in Dundee University Library).
52. LOWSON, Alexander. The tales legends and traditions of Forfarshire.
    Forfar 1891.
53. LUNAN, Rev. George B. Lessons in literature: an address delivered at the
    opening of the Newtyle Literary Society, 27 October 1880.
54. LYTHE, S. G. E. and others. The Dundee and Newtyle Railway.
    ('The Railway Magazine,' 1951).
55. LYTHE, S. G. E. The origin and development of Dundee: a study in historical
    geography. ('Scottish Geographical Magazine,' v.54. November 1938).
56. LYTHE, S. G. E. Three Dundonians. Abertay Hist. Society, 1968.
    (Includes James Carmichael, engine-builder).

57. McGIBBON and ROSS. Castellated architecture of Scotland. 1887-92.
58. MacGREGOR, M. and A. G. Midland valley of Scotland. H.M.S.O., 1936.
    (British Regional Geologies).
59. MacINTOSH, Alexander, ed. The muster roll of the Forfarshire or Lord
    Ogilvy's Regiment raised on behalf of the Royal House of Stuart in
    1745-6. 1914.
60. MacKINNON, James. The social and industrial history of Scotland. 1921.
61. McPHERSON, J. G. Strathmore, past and present. Perth, 1885.

62. MARSHALL, William. Historic scenes in Forfarshire. 1875.
63. MEIGLE W.R.I. Our Meigle book. Dundee, 1932.
64. MILLAR, Alexander Hastie. Scottish burgh life. 1903.
65. MYLES, James. Rambles in Forfarshire. 1875.

66. NATIONAL REGISTER OF ARCHIVES (Scotland). Archives in possession
    of the Newtyle Village Committee. 1974.
67. NEWTYLE AND DISTRICT HORTICULTURAL SOCIETY. Exhibition
    schedules. 1962 to date.
68. NEWTYLE BOWLING CLUB. Minutes of meetings: 16 April 1910 to
    4 February 1971. Ms.

69. NEWTYLE CHURCH. Centenary year 1972. Historical record, compiled by
     C. G. Ballantine. Typescript.
70. NEWTYLE CURLING CLUB. Minutes: 6 January 1857 to 4 February 1907. Ms.
71. NEWTYLE CURLING CLUB. Articles and list of members, 1840-1850. Ms.
72. NEWTYLE FREE CHURCH. Imperial bazaar: Kinnaird Hall, Dundee,
     15, 16 and 17 March 1900. Bazaar book.
73. NEWTYLE MAGAZINE. February 1964 to date. Typescript.
74. NEWTYLE PARISH COUNCIL. Minute book, 1926-1930. Ms.
75. NEWTYLE PAROCHIAL BOARD. Minute books, 1845-1895. 2 vols. Ms.
76. NEWTYLE PUBLIC LIBRARY.
          Minute book, 1881-1926.
          Treasurer's book, 1856-1880.
          Regulations and catalogues.
          Treasurer's book, 1881-1969.
          List of members, 1960-69.
          Receipts, 1905-1966.
          Cash book, 1856-1880.
          List of books issued, 1873-1936.
77. NEWTYLE PUBLIC PARK TRUSTEES.
          Minutes of meetings, 1905-1966.
          Treasurer's book, 1907-1966.
          Documents relating to feu charters, etc.
78. NEWTYLE SCHOOL BOARD.
          Minute book, 1873-1919.
          Letter book, 1905-1909.
79. NEWTYLE SCHOOL MANAGEMENT COMMITTEE.
          Minute book, 1919-1947.
80. NEWTYLE SECONDARY SCHOOL. Official opening, 1963.
81. NEWTYLE TENNIS CLUB. Minutes, 1947-1967.
82. NEWTYLE VILLAGE COMMITTEE. Centenary Art Exhibition catalogue,
     1972. (Typescript).
83. NEWTYLE VILLAGE COMMITTEE. Minute book, 1953-70. Ms.
84. NORRIE, W. Dundee celebrities of the 19th century. 1873.
     (George Kinloch: James Carmichael; Dr. Adam Moon).

85. OCHTERLONY, John. Account of the shire of Forfar, c1682.
     Re-printed by Forfar & District Historical Society, 1969.
86. ORDNANCE SURVEY, Archaeological branch. Original name books.

87. PENNANT, Thomas. A tour of Scotland. 1769.
88. PERKINS, John. Steam trains to Dundee, 1831-1863. Dundee Museum. 1975.
89. PLAYFAIR, James. Description of Scotland. 1819.
90. PRIVY COUNCIL. Reports to the Committee on the Dundee-Newtyle Railway.
     1841-5.

91. RAMSAY, John S. Highways and byways of Strathmore and the northern glens.
     Blairgowrie, 1927.
92. REID, Alan. Picturesque Forfarshire (1905). (Shire series).

93. SALMOND, J. B., ed. The muster roll of Angus, South African war, 1899-1900.
     Arbroath, 1900.
94. SCOTS MAGAZINE. June 1974. August 1975.
95. SCOTT, Hew. Fasti ecclesiae Scoticanae. 1925-1961.
96. SCOTTISH HISTORICAL SOCIETY. v.8. 1st series. List of persons concerned
     in the rebellion . . . 7 May 1746. 1890.
97. Same. v.9. 3rd series. Miscellany. 1926.
98. Same. v.10. Miscellany. 1965.
99. Same. v.43. Scottish population statistics. 1952.
100. 'SCOTTISH HOME & COUNTRY' (Magazine of S.W.R.I.). Articles by
      J. K. Milne in July 1974; January 1975; February 1975.
101. STATISTICAL ACCOUNT OF SCOTLAND. Newtyle.
          First, 1792.
          Second, 1842.
          Third, 1967.
102. STEEL, George McLennan. Dundee's iron horses. 1974.

103. STEVENSON, Robert. Report relative to railway from the Ports of Perth, Arbroath and Montrose. 1827.
104. STUART, John. Sculptured stones of Scotland. 2 vols. 1856-67.

105. TAYLOR, David Bethune. Archaeology of Tayside. Dundee Museum. c1959.
106. TENNANT, Charles. The radical laird: a biography of George Kinloch, 1775-1833. 1970.
107. TRANTER, Nigel. The eastern counties. 1972.
108. TRANTER, Nigel. The fortified house in Scotland. v.4. 1966.

109. VALENTINE, Easton S. Forfarshire. 1915.
110. VALUATION ROLL for Forfarshire. (Newtyle section) 1822 to date.

111. WAINWRIGHT, F. T. Souterrains of Southern Pictland. 1963.
112. WALKER, Frederick. Tayside geology. Dundee Museum. 1961.
113. WARDEN, Alex J. Angus or Forfarshire. 5 vols. 1885.
114. 'WEEKLY NEWS.' Railway supplement. 5 November 1898.
115. WHARNCLIFFE, Earl of. Abstract of accounts of the estates in Angus and Perthshire, and of other monies, from 1750 to 1770. Ms.
116. WHARNCLIFFE, Earl of. Sale catalogue of Belmont estate in the counties of Perth and Forfar. 1872.
117. WHARNCLIFFE muniments. Various papers in Sheffield Public Libraries.
118. WHISHAW, Francis. The railways of Great Britain and Ireland. 1840.
119. WILSON, Sir Daniel. Prehistoric annals of Scotland. 1851.
120. WOOD, Nicholas. Report to the Committee of Management relative to the Dundee and Newtyle Railway. Dundee, 1832.

121. The Dundee, Perth and Cupar Advertiser ⎫ Dates
122. The Dundee Courier ⎪ are given
123. The Evening Telegraph ⎬ in
124. The People's Journal ⎭ the text.

Additional items:

125. CAMPERDOWN, George Duncan, 4th Earl of. (1845-1933). Memories of Camperdown, Lundie and some others. Ms. (incl. Old Tay Bridge; Dundee/Newtyle Railway; Watt engine).
126. CARRIE, John. Ancient things in Angus. 1881.
127. FLETT, J. F. & T. M. Traditional dancing in Scotland. 1964.
128. SHAW, W. J. Inscriptions on the pre-1855 headstones at Newtyle, Angus, Parish burial ground. 1977 (typed).
129. GUNTHER, A. E. William Carmichael M'Intosh, F.R.S. (St Andrews University publications No. LXI), 1977.
130. MUIR, Augustus, and DAVIES, Mair. A Victorian shipowner: a portrait of Sir Charles Cayzer, Bt. (1843-1916). 1978.
131. DOUGLAS, Sir James. The Scots Peerage.
132. Scottish History Society. Dundee textile industry, 1790-1885. 1969.

INDEX

page

'Aggieside' (right-of-way)   65
Agriculture   53-64
ARDLER 9; 73; 75
Armed services 31; 40
AUCHTERTYRE 1; 3; 5; 6; 11
         farm 56; 58
         quarry   65

BALCRAIG 5; 6; 11
BALLANTINE, Charles 45; 84
BALMAIN—see BALMAW
BALMAW 6; 11-12
Banking   98-99
BANNATYNE HOUSE 6; 12-14
BANNATYNE Home Farm 8; 58
BARTY, Thomas   25
BEATON, Miss Marjorie   44; 45; 46
BEVERLEY, Maxwell 101; 103
BILLENDEN   5
BLACK, Rev. Thomas   23
Blacksmith—see Smiddy
Bone Mill (Chemical Works) 45; 70
Bowling Club   89-90
Boy Scouts   85
BOYD, Maister Robert   23
BRIGGS, Messrs.   65
BRIGGS, Miss Nettie   88
British Legion   86
British Red Cross Society   86-87
BROWSTER, George, teacher   38
BURMAN, David Clark 71; 103
BURNETT, John   64
         Mervyn, E. H.   64
BURNMOUTH 6; 59
BURNSIDE   59
         Quarry 1; 65
BUTCHART, John, slater, Kirkinch   39
BUTE, Countess of   7

Cafes—see Refreshment Rooms
Canals   80-81
CARMICHAEL Brothers   72
Cattle Dealers   102
CAYZER, Lady 20; 86; 89
         Sir Charles W. 20; 86; 92; 93
         Sir James   20
Cemetery   28
CHALMERS, Rev. John   25
CHRISTIE, John (1690), teacher   38
Church   23-28
         Episcopalian   28
         Free 26-27; 45
         Tokens   27
         United Presbyterian   25-26

		page
Churchyard	....	27-28
CLEPHANE, Rev. George	....	25
Coal dealers	....	102
Commercial Inn (Hotel)	....	101
COLVIN, William W.	....	48; 84; 96
Courts, Barons'	....	6-8
COUSTON farm and house	....	59
Cricket	....	90
CROOKSTON Farm	....	59
CUNNINGHAM, Rev. John MacPherson	....	25
Curling	....	90-92
DALGAIRNS, Andrew, of Ingliston	....	8; 69; 101
Dancing	....	82-83
DAVIDSTON Farm	....	60
DENEND Farm	....	60
DENOON Castle	....	4
Distilling	....	71
Doctors	....	102
Drama	....	84
DRUMKILBO	....	69
DUNCAN, George, 4th Earl of Camperdown	....	77
DUNDEE and Newtyle Railway	....	72-80
EASSON, John	....	57
EDDERTY Farm	....	60
Education	....	38-52
FENWICK, James	....	52
FERGUSSON, Peter, headmaster	....	40; 41
FINDLAY, Alexander	....	57
Fishwife	....	98
Flax—see Linen		
FLEMING, Rev. John	....	26
FLORIDEW, Rev. Mr.	....	20
Gas Works	....	70
Geology	....	1
Girl Guides	....	85; 86
Golf	....	92-94
Good Templars, Kinpurney Lodge	....	40
GRAY, David (hermit)	....	19-20
John & Sons	....	39; 65
Robert, Innkeeper	....	99; 101
Halls	....	84-85
HALTOUN—see HATTON		
HARDIE, David, blacksmith	....	39
HATTON, Castle	....	5; 6; 14-17
Farm	....	60
HENDERSTON Farm	....	61
HENRY, John	....	41; 42; 70; 78; 104
Robert	....	84
HILL, David, of Bannatyne House	....	34; 70; 91; 102
Mrs Jean	....	104
HONEYMAN, Thomas	....	82
Hotel—see Commercial Inn		
Housing	....	31-32
Inns	....	99; 101
IRVINE, William, headmaster	....	37; 46-47; 51

		page
JACK, John	....	10; 31; 34; 35; 36; 39; 41; 42; 43; 45; 48; 49; 50; 51; 101; 104
'Jam factory'	....	69; 70
JAMIESON, Mrs Margaret	....	86
JOHNSTONE, Dr. Hugh	....	102
JOINER, Miss Ella	....	86
Henry, headmaster	....	47-48
Joiners	....	101
KEILLOR Farm	....	6; 17-18; 61-62
Stone	....	4
KERR, Christopher, writer	....	8
KINLOCH, George, of Kinloch	....	72-73
KINPURNEY Farm	....	5; 6; 62
Quarry	....	65
Tower	....	18-20
KINPURNIE Castle	....	20
KIRKINCH	....	1; 20-21; 69
KIRKTON Farm	....	6; 58; 62-63
KYNPRONY—see KINPURNEY		
LAMOND, David	....	79-80
Sir William	....	105
William Bradley	....	80; 105-106
LANDALE, Charles	....	72
Laundry	....	101
Library—Newtyle Public Library	....	48-52; 84
Linen	....	67-70
Literary Society, Newtyle	....	40; 84
Lochee weavers	....	48; 67
Looms and loomshops	....	10; 69-70
LUNAN, Rev. George Bell	....	25; 51; 84
MACDONALD, William R.	....	86; 93
M'INTOSH, Professor	....	89; 106
MACKENZIE, Rev. Alexander	....	23
Sir George	....	6
James—see WHARNCLIFFE		
MANN, father and sons, quarriers	....	65
Masons (builders)	....	101
MATHEWSON, George	....	8
MAXWELL, Rev. William	....	26
MECHIE, Rev. John	....	26; 51
MEIGLE	....	5; 69
Mill of Newtyle	....	5-8; 71; 101
MILLER, Rev. Edward	....	26
MILLHOLE Farm	....	6; 57; 63
Quarry	....	65
MILLS, Dr. David Marnie	....	35; 46; 102
Molecatchers	....	101
MONTROSE, Marquis of	....	3; 11; 15
MOON, George, linen manufacturer	....	35; 69; 91
Rev. John	....	25
MORGAN, James D., headmaster	....	41-48; 51
MUIR, Rev. John	....	26
MUNDAMALLA House	....	21
Music	....	41; 82-83
NAIRNE, Mr, of Drumkilbo	....	9; 21; 69; 75
NETHERMILL	....	63

	page
NEWBIGGING	6; 21-22
Farm	63
Newtyle Bulb & Farming Co.	64; 70
NEWTYLE Castle—see HATTON Castle	
Newtyle Chemical Co.	70
Newtyle & Coupar Angus Railway	74-75
Newtyle & District Horticultural Society	88
Newtyle Dramatic Society	84
Newtyle & Glammis Railway	74-75
Newtyle Literary Society	40; 84
Newtyle Musical Society	82
Newtyle Public Library—see Library	
Newtyle Village, beginning	8-10
OGILVIE, Miss Isabella	97
OLIPHANTS	5; 6; 14-17
Packmen	98; 101
Parish Council	37
Park	96-97
Parochial Board	33-37
PATULLO, Rev. George	23
PITCUR	3
PITNAPPIE Farm	63; 64
Quarry	65
PLAYFAIR, Prof. James	19
Police	31
POLLOCK, John H.	84
Poor—see Poverty	
Population	30-31
Post Office	99
Poverty	29-30; 33-37
PRIVY'S PRAP	20
Pterapsis Mitchelli	1
Pupil teachers	40
Putting	94
Quarries	64-65
Quoits	94-95
Rabbit-trappers	101
RALSTON Farm	64
Red Cross—see British Red Cross Society	
Refreshment rooms (cafes)	99
REID, John ('Dancie')	44; 82-83
Roads	81; 102
ROBERTSON, Mr, teacher	38; 47
Romans	3
ROY, Miss V., teacher	47
Rural, The—see Women's Rural Institute	
SAUNDERS, James, millowner	71
SAUNDERS, Thomas	101
Sawmill	101
School—enlarging, 1875	39-40
Board	38-46
House	43; 47
Management Committee	46-48
Sewage	32-33
SHEPHERD, Robert & Mrs	85-86
Shops	98-101
SIM, Ernest	84
Robert	21
William	21

	page
SIMPSON, Miss, Alyth	97
William	88
SINCLAIR, R. B., banker	85
Slaters	101
SMALL, Rev. Alexander	25
Smiddy, Newtyle	7; 101
SMITH, Dr. Alex Gillespie	102
Rev. Robert	25
Social life	29-37
Souterrains	3
'Spec Knowes'	1
STEELE, R. W. & I.	65
STEVENSON, Eliza K., teacher	38-39; 44
STRATHEARN, David	91
TEMPLETON Farm	62
Tennis	95-96
Thane Stane	4
THOMAS, Major, of Bannatyne House	14; 70
Tinkers	98
Toll-house	81; 102
Tylds	1
'V nteers' (8th Forfarshire Rifles)	31; 40; 102
WAINWRIGHT, Dr. F. T.	3
WASHINGTON (village)—see ARDLER	
Water supply	32
Street wells	10
WATSON, Hugh	11; 13; 55; 56-57
WATT, John	86
WEDDERSPOON, Thomas, of Castleton	46; 89
WHARNCLIFFE, Earl of	8; 12-13 18-20; 69
WHARNCI FFE HALL—see HALLS	
WHITTON, Andrew, of Couston	33; 37; 42; 44; 49; 85; 89
WILSON, James, headmaster	33-35; 38; 39; 40; 43; 50; 91
WINN, Sergeant, instructor	44
Women's Rural Institute	87-88
WOOD, Rev. Robert	26
Youth clubs	85